MW01070046

TABLE OF CONTENTS

Top 20 Test Taking Tips

1. Carefully follow all the test registration procedures
2. Know the test directions, duration, topics, question types, how many questions
3. Setup a flexible study schedule at least 3-4 weeks before test day
4. Study during the time of day you are most alert, relaxed, and stress free
5. Maximize your learning style; visual learner use visual study aids, auditory learner use auditory study aids
6. Focus on your weakest knowledge base
7. Find a study partner to review with and help clarify questions
8. Practice, practice, practice
9. Get a good night's sleep; don't try to cram the night before the test
10. Eat a well balanced meal
11. Know the exact physical location of the testing site; drive the route to the site prior to test day
12. Bring a set of ear plugs; the testing center could be noisy
13. Wear comfortable, loose fitting, layered clothing to the testing center; prepare for it to be either cold or hot during the test
14. Bring at least 2 current forms of ID to the testing center
15. Arrive to the test early; be prepared to wait and be patient
16. Eliminate the obviously wrong answer choices, then guess the first remaining choice
17. Pace yourself; don't rush, but keep working and move on if you get stuck
18. Maintain a positive attitude even if the test is going poorly
19. Keep your first answer unless you are positive it is wrong
20. Check your work, don't make a careless mistake

Student Development and Learning

Erikson's stages of social-emotional development

1. Learning Basic Trust vs. Basic Mistrust: The period of infancy in the first years of life where children who are loved and cared for develop trust and security. Children who are not become mistrustful and insecure.
2. Learning Autonomy vs. Shame: This occurs during early childhood, where the well-loved child welcomes his new sense of control, manifesting itself in tantrums, possessiveness, and the "no" and "mine" stage.
3. Learning Initiative vs. Guilt: A healthy child, usually up to school age, will develop his imagination, cooperate with others, and be both a leader and follower. A child who feels guilt will be fearful, not quite fit in socially, be dependent on adults, and have an underdeveloped imagination.
4. Industry vs. Inferiority: Entering school and up to junior high, the child will learn formal skills of life, initiate rules into free play, and desire self-discipline.
5. Learning Identity vs. Identity Diffusion: From adolescence to late teens, the child answers the question as to who he is, after possibly going through rebellions and self-doubt. He may experiment with different roles, but anticipate achievement instead of feeling paralyzed by this process.
6. Learning Intimacy vs. Isolation: A successful young adult pursues true intimacy, whether it is in the form of long-lasting and enduring friendships or a partner for marriage.
7. Learning Generativity vs. Self-Absorption: Once adulthood is reached, whether in marriage or parenthood, the sense of working cooperatively and productively becomes of the utmost importance, rather than focusing only on independent goals.
8. Integrity vs. Despair: Once all other seven steps have been resolved, the mature adult reaches adjustment integrity. He can experiment after working hard and has developed a self-concept of which makes him happy and is proud of what he has created.

Mental retardation

Mental retardation is a term that is used when people have abnormal limitations on their levels of mental functioning. These could be in communicating, taking care of themselves and social skills. Due to these limitations, their development has been altered and they will develop at a slower rate than most children. Learning to speak and walk, as well as dressing themselves and eating will take longer to acquire. They are still able to learn, but often require more time and more assistance in order for this to take place. There may be things, such as abstract concepts, that they will never be able to fully comprehend. About 10% the students receiving special education in schools have some form of mental retardation.

Causes of mental retardation

1. Perinatal problems: These are problems that occur during labor and birth, such as the baby not receiving enough oxygen when it is born.

2. Problems during pregnancy: Mental retardation can occur when the conditions in the womb are altered in some way when the baby is developing. For example, if a woman drinks or uses drugs during pregnancy, or gets a serious infection.
3. Genetic conditions: This occurs when both parents have abnormalities in their genes; for example, Down syndrome is a genetic condition.
4. Health problems: Exposure to certain diseases such as the measles or meningitis can cause mental retardation. Also, extreme malnutrition or exposure to poisons, such as arsenic or mercury can also cause problems.

Kolb's learning process

Kolb outlined four stages that occur when learning is taking place. It begins at any stage and is continuous, meaning that there is no limit to the number of times each stage is experienced. These stages define learning as occurring through concrete experience, observation and reflection, abstract conceptualization, or active experimentation. As we have more experience at being learners, we tend to start at the same stage for all of our learning processes. For example, a student might come up with an idea for a science fair project (abstract conceptualization), and then proceed to experiment with different ways of presenting the information (active experimentation), then create the final product (concrete experience) and write up the report to accompany the project (observation and reflection). Depending on each person's learning style, they may start at a different stage every time, or stick with the one that works best for them after repeated successes.

Reg Revans' theory of Action Learning

Reg Revans' theory of Action Learning is an approach that uses small cooperative learning groups. These groups meet regularly with each other to discuss real-life issues. The aim of these groups is to learn from one another and with each other through the experiences that they share. He believed that action and learning must coincide for the other to exist. By having small groups, possibly ones that students choose in order to feel comfortable, they can develop a rapport and a safe environment in order for these learning sessions to take place. He believed that these groups were successful in finding solutions for problems that do not necessarily have a right or wrong answer, but can benefit from having other individuals and their subjective experiences with whom to discuss a problem.

Constructivism and behaviorism

Behaviorism
Learning is defined as simply the new behavior that we acquire through experiences. It focuses mainly on observable behaviors, such as social interactions or physical exertions, not mental activities or thought processes. These two things are not the focus because they cannot be quantified and therefore cannot be measured in the same ways that observable behavior can.

Constructivism
Based on the understanding that due to all of our experiences we construct our own comprehension of the world we live in. We each all create our own mental rules and values to make sense of the experiences we have. Therefore, learning is simply how we adjust our "rules" to include new experiences, which may in turn cause us to reassess our mental rules.

Piaget's and Vygotsky's respective learning theories

Piaget created a model of child development and learning that shows how their cognitive structure develops. It is based around the main idea that children build cognitive structures or concepts in order to respond to experiences in their environment. It also becomes more complex as it develops, explaining how children move from simple movements, such as sucking their thumb, to complex mental activities such as reading as they become older.

Vygotsky thought that culture is the main influencing factor on human development and thus created the social cognition learning model. Because humans are the only species to have created culture, every child develops within this context. This culture that influences the development of the child starts with the family environment, but then spreads to the media, school and community.

Piaget's developmental stages for children

1. Sensorimotor (birth to 2 years of age): Children build their set of concepts through physical interaction with their environment. They do not have the sense of object permanence that whereas to them it appears that the toy train ceases to exist when it is out of their sight, the toy train still exists.
2. Preoperational stage (ages 2-7): They still operate better in concrete situations. Although they may recognize abstract concepts, they are still unable to fully grasp them and their existence.
3. Concrete operations (ages 7-11): With more physical experiences, they can start to conceptualize, and may be able to solve abstract problems, such as using numbers in math instead of adding and subtracting physical objects.
4. Formal Operations (begins at 11-15): At this stage, children's cognitive structures are like those of an adult and include conceptual reasoning.

Cultural and social development of children

Culture provides the medium from which most children acquire their knowledge. Also, culture gives children a chance to put their knowledge into experience. Therefore, culture can teach children both what and how to think. Children learn most of their experiences through interaction with someone else, namely parents or teachers, but sometimes siblings and peers. Eventually, children assume the responsibility of solving problems for themselves and not relying on others for help. Language is the main way in which these transactions take place and therefore language is important in both the social and cultural development, because through it are conveyed many hidden messages about what is acceptable both culturally and socially; for example, swearing is not allowed in a school culture, but may be viewed highly in a social setting of other children. It is mainly through personal experience that the differences are determined for each child.

Perception disabilities

Perception disabilities occur when there is an interruption in the input process from the eyes or ears to the neurons in the brain. These disabilities are different than someone who is near- or farsighted, or who has hearing problems. The two main groups of perception disabilities are visual and auditory. Visual perception can be affected in three ways: figure-ground, depth perception or visual-motor.

These mainly affect how a child processes information, and may have cause a child to have trouble reading or affect their gross motor skills. These children may have trouble judging the distance between themselves and other objects, and have difficulties with sports that require quick hand-eye coordination. Children with auditory perception difficulties may have trouble determining the differences between sounds in language. Or they may have difficulty hearing a voice in a room with many voices and appear to not be paying attention.

How a child with a sensory perception disorder would behave

A sensory perception disorder is one with which any tactile activity can cause discomfort and even pain. Some children are particularly sensitive to touch and this is usually discovered early on, when, as an infant, he will not like being touched or held.

In a classroom, he may be fidgety, complaining of the tag on his shirt or rearranging clothes or his shoes. He will not want to sit too close to anyone in classroom, thus requiring a specific place in any classroom seating place. He may appear to be anti-social because he hovers around the edges of groups, seeming to not want to join in, or be too shy to do so.

How learning disabilities develop

A learning disability is a disorder of the brain. It occurs when the way the information transmitted in the brain does so a little differently. It does not mean that the brain is damaged, but rather that when the brain was in its earliest stage of development that something affected it. The four main parts of the brain most often affected are language skills, muscle skills, thinking skills and organization

skills. A person with difficulty with language may struggle with reading or writing. Someone with a muscle skill disability may have problems with catching a ball or judging depth and distance. A thinking skills disability may affect problem solving or processing information. Many children with an organizational disability have trouble keeping track of their possessions and assignments.

Attention deficit hyperactivity disorder (ADHD)

ADHD is classified by inappropriate amounts of inattention, impulsiveness and hyperactivity. All three behaviors do not need to exist in order for a child to be diagnosed with ADHD. Hyperactivity is usually defined as being fidgety, squirmy or restless on a regular basis. Inattention occurs when they are distracted by both visual and auditory stimuli. They also may daydream and be distracted by other thoughts or ideas easily and have trouble sustaining a conversation. Impulsiveness shows when children seem to be unable to think before they act, therefore they have trouble learning from previous experiences and will tend to repeat undesirable behavior such as calling out, or becoming physical and grabbing a pencil or hitting another child.

Diagnosis and treatment process of ADHD

There are many symptoms of ADHD that are common with children and adolescents and therefore it can be difficult to make an accurate diagnosis since there is not one fool-proof way of assessing ADHD. Usually, ADHD is declared using five steps, outlined in the DSM-IV-TR. Teachers may be given forms that have certain criteria of behavior on them, and give their point of view on the behavior seen over the past six months. This is usually compared with the clinical

- 8 -

and family histories, after which a diagnosis can be made. Treatments for ADHD include both medication and non-medication methods. There are a wide variety of drugs for the treatment of ADHD, and the level of success depends on the individual child. Non-medication treatment could include therapy, and small group help at school once the school is aware of the diagnosis.

Multicultural education

Multicultural education is education that sees to enrich each student's perspective by valuing pluralism and studying a variety of cultures. It seeks to lessen prejudices and increase tolerance, and ensure that minority students are receiving a fair and equal education. It does not believe in the analogy of the melting pot, where all cultures blend together, but celebrates the differences and aims instead for a "mixed salad" where individual cultures are distinct from each other, but form a unique whole as they are put together. It accepts and praises the differences in the individual and tries to project that there is not a typical American, but that everyone who lives here is American.

Criticisms of multicultural education

Some criticisms of multicultural education are concerned about the potential damage that pluralism could have on schools. They fear that many common traditions, values and purposes may be eradicated because of the focus on other cultures and traditions. The main idea that some critics would have is that multicultural education teaches that everything is of equal value and that the schools have a responsibility to teach about all of these values. It is also judged as a reform movement against the discrimination of students who are discriminated against because of their language, race, religion, sex, or age.

How multicultural backgrounds affect learning

Nonwhite students now comprise 1/3 of the under-18 population in the US. The recent growth is especially large in Latino and Asian populations; two populations which within themselves are extremely diverse. This will cause continued growth in the number of students who enter school who are ELL and whose family backgrounds may not correlate with the norms and expectations schools may have. Many of these children will succeed in school and adapt successfully to the school culture. If ELL students do not acquire English to a satisfactory level, their language barrier may cause them to have low levels of achievement and eventually even cause them to drop out of school altogether. Having family support is important for any student to succeed in school, but if the parents do not speak English at all, then it can be difficult for their children to succeed as well.

Reinforcement in learning and behavior

Reinforcement explains that behavior is a function of its consequences, meaning that a student will repeat a certain behavior, such as raising his hand to answer a question if the consequences are desirable, such as positive reinforcement from the teacher about his answer. This could be either a verbal response, such as "That was a great answer," or points that lead to extra credit or a tangible reward. It is important that the reward is something that is of interest to the student in order for this model to be effective. On the other hand, if an inappropriate behavior, such as calling out, is given a positive reinforcement, such as attention from the teacher, instead of negative reinforcement, such as the teacher ignoring the student, then the student will continue with the undesirable behavior. Criticism of this theory includes that it is too rigid and quantifies human behavior instead of qualifying it.

Operant conditioning interpretations of learning

Studying his operant conditioning interpretations of learning may help teachers learn why some students react positively to certain subjects and why they will dislike others. Some students will enter a certain class, like art, with excitement and ready to learn, whereas some will enter the classroom reluctantly. This is due to past experiences. The student who loves art may have had positive experiences with previous art teachers, and another student may not have. Skinner would argue that the student who loves art is that way because of a number of positive experiences that have reinforced that love of art. A student who does not like art feels that way because of a series of negative experiences, not necessarily because he is poor at the subject.

Persuasive Models Social Learning theory

This theory starts with the assertion that individuals will pay attention to positive experiences that they observe and strive to repeat the same experience themselves. This is where consistency is important in a classroom because students will often expect the same response for an observed behavior. This could manifest itself in several ways. A student who admires a teacher of a subject may work hard to please the teacher and to become like them because he sees the teacher as a role model. Students may strive to achieve high grades like those of their classmates if they overhear them talking about how they get paid for good grades. If a student repeats the same behavior of a previous student but gets a different reward, or none at all, the student will continue to be unclear about what the teacher wants from his students.

Cognitive view of motivation

The cognitive view of motivation believes that behavior is influenced by the way that people think about themselves and the environment in which they are. There are four influences that explain how the direction of this behavior takes place. The first is the intrinsic need to have a logically constructed knowledge base, which means that people need to make sense of their experiences. Knowing what one's expectations are for completing a task successfully is the second influence, because there needs to be a certain amount of self-awareness in order to react positively to an occurrence and repeat the experience. The third influence are the factors that one believes account for success and failure, such as education and perseverance, and the fourth is one's belief about his own ability to solve problems and think critically.

Impact of cooperative learning on motivation

Classroom tasks can be set so that students are competing with one another, working individually, or cooperating with others in order to receive the awards that teachers make available for completing the work. Usually, competitive arrangements are used, which means that each student is competing against each other for the best grade. However, cooperative arrangements have an overall better result when students are meant to be working with each other toward a common goal. The benefits of this system tend to be qualitative and may be difficult to measure, because often the real-life experiences students gain by working with each other outweighs all other benefits in the long run.

Achievement behavior as defined by Atkinson

Atkinson believed that differences in achievement behavior are due to the differences in the need for achievement that each person feels. He thought that the desire for achievement was a global desire, and one that sought to achieve recognition or competence. This idea is reinforcement by both intrinsic and extrinsic factors. People who have a high need for achievement tend to be more focused on the possible success than the possible failure. On the other hand, people who have a low need for achievement tend to stop before they even start because their feel of failure outweighs any belief that they will succeed. Therefore all students should be encouraged to participate and challenge themselves in order to have as many positive experiences as possible.

Prior knowledge

Prior knowledge is a combination of one's attitudes, experiences and knowledge which already exist. Attitudes can range from beliefs about ourselves as learners or being aware of our own strengths and weaknesses. It can also be our level of motivation and responsibility for our own learning. The experiences from our daily activities, especially ones with our friends and families, give us a background from which we derive most of our understanding. Individual events in our lives provide us experiences from which to draw from; both bad and good and influence how we deal with future situations. This knowledge is drawn from a wide variety of things, from knowledge of specific content areas and the concepts within, to the goals that we have for ourselves academically.

Appropriate and accurate prior knowledge

It is important that students have accurate and relevant prior knowledge to be used. If prior knowledge is inaccurate, it could negatively affect their performance. A student who has little or no prior knowledge will almost certainly perform better than a student with inaccurate prior knowledge. Accessing prior knowledge can cause awkward situations, especially if students bring up issues that teachers are unable to control and that may be inappropriate and prejudiced. However, using students' prior knowledge can help them to reexamine their current understandings and test their old knowledge with new facts and figures. Prior knowledge must be activated and providing a safe classroom where students feel safe to express their opinions is the first step in having this be successful.

Activating prior knowledge

There are several specific methods that teachers can use to activate the prior knowledge of their students. This is important because some students may have valuable prior knowledge but may not be aware of it if it hasn't been activated properly. One way to activate this knowledge is by a word association task. Writing a term on the board at the beginning of a new unit, such as slavery, can be a good way to see what students associate with the term. It is also a beneficial way for the teacher to see what the students already know and plan the unit accordingly. Another way is to use analogies or figures of speech that the students may use without even knowing it. Before introducing a novel, for example, the students could examine the analogy "The straw that broke the camel's back" and then study a novel where that is the main theme.

Anticipating students' preconceptions

Preconceptions are opinions or conceptions formed before adequate knowledge or experience has been accessed. They are often prejudices or biases. Students' preconceptions will often come into the classroom, especially in learner-centered ones. It can only be helpful to integrate these preconceptions into what is studied instead of ignoring them altogether. Firstly, teachers should pay attention to the knowledge that students are bringing into the classroom and be aware of cultural differences. If teachers remain attentive to students' individual progress, then they will be able to fill in the blanks of where the student has gaps in their knowledge due to their preconceptions. It may be useful to provide basic knowledge before a topic is studied and then discuss students' reactions in order to talk about preconceptions and have students recognize that they exist.

How preconceptions affect the teaching of culture

Culture is an aspect of everything that is taught, whether or not teachers are aware of it. The gestures, words and objects used while teaching are all a part of culture. It is important that culture is taught without judgment and that there is not a value placed on one culture over another in the classroom. This is primarily because culture, especially American culture, is not monolithic; cultures require interaction amongst different cultures in order for humans to survive. Similarly, there is a classroom culture that could be much different for most students, and therefore it is important to assess students' preconceptions of classrooms because the rules between each room differ with the teacher.

Recognizing attention deficit disorder

Teachers should have little trouble identifying those students who may be suffering from attention deficit disorder, as the behavior of these students will probably be disruptive. Students with ADD usually make careless mistakes in their work and have a hard time sustaining their attention during long lecture periods. They are typically disorganized and are often losing things. They may fidget a great deal with their hands, and just seem to have a great deal of nervous energy. They often talk too much and out of turn. They often have a difficult time working quietly and keeping their hands off of the other students. Many students are so afflicted by attention deficit disorder that they almost seem to be possessed, or driven by some internal motor.

Maslow's hierarchy of human needs

Maslow believed that our most basic needs must be met before we satisfy higher levels of human potential. The first four levels are the deficiency motives that must be reached before the final, fifth, level. The basic level contains our physiological needs, such as food, water and shelter. Once these are satisfied, the next level to be achieved is freedom from danger and a life that is stable and anxiety-free. The third level has more to do with behavior that strives for positive relationships that give a sense of love and belonging. As the three lower levels of motivation are satisfied, then feelings of confidence and self-respect fuel one's self-esteem. The final level, a growth motive, is self-actualization when one's potential is realized and self-direction comes to follow. Teachers can assess where their students fall on the hierarchy and use that knowledge to better deal with their students as individuals.

William Glasser's control theory

The control theory describes how our motivations, behaviors and actions are attempts to satisfy needs such as love, survival, power and freedom. If we are able to understand these needs and how we try to pursue them, then we can choose on how best to meet them. When teachers use this intrinsic motivation with their students, the result can be that students see how they feel when work is completed, and strive to always improve themselves. Many students express that their favorite part of going to school is being with their friends (a built-in need) and therefore group work, or cooperative learning, can satisfy this need instead of independent seatwork or teacher lectures. Cooperative learning can end inappropriate behaviors that are seeking power, and instead work of the concept that in small groups, students will be listening to each other, which will in turn foster a sense of self-respect and importance.

Sensory stimulation theory

When the senses are stimulated, effective learning can take place. That is the basic definition of sensory stimulation theory. The most effective medium of learning takes place through seeing; this could be by watching a performance of a text done as a play; or watching an experiment conducted by a teacher before the students attempt it themselves. Hearing something is the next most effective way of learning something, and the other senses—smell, taste and touch—all have about the same effectiveness after the others when they are used in learning. The most important part of this theory is that when more than one sense is stimulated—ideally more than two—it is then that the most effective type of learning takes place. This is also along the same lines of multiple intelligences, which states that students have more than one type of intelligence that should be used when teaching.

Gestalt approach, Holistic learning theory, and the humanistic approach to learning

The Gestalt approach (also known as the cognitive approach) gives experience the most importance in this learning theory because it believes that through active problem-solving insights will develop which are vital to learning because each student approaches each task subjectively and will therefore develop insights that make sense to them individually.

Holistic learning theory
This theory takes into account that each student has a different personality comprised of many different elements, such as imaginations, feelings and intelligence, that all need to be stimulated if learning is to be achieved.

The humanistic approach (facilitation theory)
This theory was developed by the work of Carl Rogers and other psychologists. It places the importance of learning upon the person who is facilitating the learning. In order for this to take place, the atmosphere of the classroom needs to be safe in order for new ideas to be explored and risks to be taken.

Classroom that follows the humanistic approach

Teachers would be willing to question their own beliefs and values, able to listen to students' experiences, ideas, and especially feelings—as concerned with the relationship with each student as well as what they were teaching—and open to both positive and negative feedback in order to examine their own behavior and teaching style.

Students are given the chance to be responsible for the content of their learning, provide their own experiences and feelings in order to be able to get the most out of what they are learning, learn that self-evaluation is an important part of their learning process and that it provides them the chance to examine their own progress in achieving results or solving problems.

Learning styles which affect how students learn and perform

Visual learners—These students learn best by seeing written directions and benefit from having notes written down on a whiteboard or overhead. They are able to extract information from written text well and benefit from having main points summarized on the board during class discussions.

Oral learners—These students perform better when information can be heard; for instance, they may prefer to read aloud or listen to someone else read aloud. Discussions can be helpful in order to hear the information once, and then repeat it to someone else.

Kinesthetic learners—These students benefit from hands-on experiences and learn best from participating in the classroom, such as conducting a science experiment.

Howard Gardner's theory of multiple intelligences

Gardner outlines eight distinct intelligences that people use in problem solving: namely, linguistic, musical, logical-mathematical, spatial, bodily-kinesthetic, naturalistic, interpersonal and intrapersonal, with a possible ninth: existential. Schools traditionally emphasize linguistic and logical-mathematical. Gardner placed emphasis upon learning skills in context, such as

apprenticeships, rather than solely by textbooks. Traditional subjects, like English and math, should be taught in ways that appeal to all the multiple intelligences. History, for example, could be taught through dramatic reenactments, biographies, and architecture. He also thought that assessments should be tailored to different abilities and that student choice with assessments would ensure that the students were completing the task to the best of their abilities and utilizing the intelligence in which they were most skilled.

Diagnosing mental retardation

The diagnosis can be made by looking at two main things: the ability of a person's brain to learn, think, problem-solve, or make sense of their surroundings, and whether the person has the skills he needs in order to live independently. The first one—intellectual functioning—can be measured by an IQ test. The average score is 100 and people who score below 75 on the test are considered to have mental retardation. To measure the second one, or their adaptive behavior, observations are done in social environments to see how the person reacts compared to others his age, such as going to the bathroom and feeding himself, as well as interacting and communicating with others.

Oppositional Defiant Disorder (ODD)

Oppositional Defiant Disorder is less common than ADHD or ADD, but is still classified as a behavioral disorder that some children will have. It is classified as consisting of behavior that is negative, defiant, disobedient and hostile toward figures of authority, such as parents, teachers or other adults, but must last for at least six months. Most behavioral disorders need to be observed for at least this period of time before they can be correctly diagnosed. The most typical ways in which an ODD manifests itself are arguing with authority figures, refusing to follow requests or directions, deliberately annoying people by becoming inappropriate, and blaming others for their actions. They do not usually include aggression towards animals or people, or actions of a destructive nature, such as vandalism or theft.

Conduct Disorder (CD)

Students who are diagnosed with a Conduct Disorder usually exhibit certain behaviors that are associated with a CD. These behaviors include an early onset of sexual behavior, smoking and drinking, as well as unnecessary risk taking. It is defined as a pattern of behavior that violates the basic rights of others, or significant social norms and rules specific to their age group. They often stay out late, run away from home, or skip school. They may physically harm other children or animals and due to this may not have many positive social interactions because they always are doing things according to their rules with little regard for others' feelings or property.

Talented and gifted (TAG) students

TAG students can be the most challenging types of students that teachers have in their classroom. Students who are gifted are extremely bright and grasp ideas readily, and even apply their own interpretations to ideas you present of which you might not even be aware. Their level of creativity is displayed in their original thinking and creations. They do have special needs, however, and can be overlooked in the classroom because they seem to be self-sufficient in acquiring the new material, but do require consideration because of their level of intelligence. Most people are slow to realize that gifted children do require special adaptations. When gifted students

are not assisted, many become dropouts or feel understimulated in school and as a result, most of our brightest and most talented students become turned off or underdeveloped.

Social and emotional issues

Adolescence is a roller coaster of a time, and these difficulties often manifest themselves in various ways in the classroom. Sexism, racism, and homophobia will often appear in many ways as the students are going through puberty and are enjoying the novelty of these issues. It is important to maintain a safe environment in any classroom, therefore these sorts of comments should not be tolerated, a fact which should be made clear from the start. Students could be dealing with any one of these issues in their home life as some parents perceive their getting older as needing more responsibilities at home. Some students will also become more rebellious and try drugs, smoking or drinking. Maintaining a mature attitude towards these topics and trying to integrate them into the curriculum is beneficial as it will provide real-life experience to the students going through any problems.

Critical thinking

Critical thinking is defined as the pursuit of relevant, reasonable and reliable knowledge about the world that is focused on what one should believe or do. Someone who is thinking critically is able to ask appropriate questions, collect information that is relevant, sort through the gathered information, develop reasoning, and come to certain conclusions through this process. Critical thinking is higher order thinking that enables someone to decide on which political candidate to vote for, assess the dangers of gun violence, and many other tasks that are studied in school. Lower-order thinking would be checking to see whether one received the correct change at a grocery store, or being able to tie ones shoes. The goal of critical thinking is to develop responsible citizens who contribute to a healthy, productive society and who don't succumb to its temptations.

Critical thinking is an important skill for all students to learn because it provides students with the tools to be successful and responsible citizens when they have finished school. Due to the fact that children are not born with the power to think critically, and that it is something which must be taught, in order to successfully educate all students this is a skill that must be aspired to. Since it is a skill that only educated instructors could possess, it is important that adequate time in school is devoted to this task. Students who are able to learn this skill will benefit by being able to question information, being able to think for themselves, challenge traditional beliefs, discover new information and investigate problems.

Critical thinking controversy

If critical thinking skills enable an individual to think for one's self and make decisions that affect one's life, it could also lead to more rebellion and challenging of authority in schools. If students are taught critical thinking skills, they may learn to not believe just any information given to them and spend all their time questioning everything, instead of it leading to some result, such as becoming more educated. As long as critical thinking is taught with the goal of some end, such as completing a project or experiment, then it is useful to teach this skill in school, and let the students decide whether it is useful to them or not.

Characteristics of a critical thinker

1. Organizes thoughts in order to be able to articulate them
2. Uses evidence relevantly and objectively
3. Only makes a judgment when all evidence has been presented
4. Understands that there are different degrees of belief
5. Sees hidden similarities and analogies
6. Learns independently
7. Applies previous knowledge to new situations to solve problems
8. Can see irrelevancies in verbal arguments and rephrase them concisely
9. Questions ones own views and attempts to assess why those views are held
10. Is sensitive to the difference between intensities and validities of beliefs
11. Is aware that one's knowledge is limited
12. Recognizes that one's opinions are not always right, that they contain bias, and that there is a danger of including personal preferences in the consideration of evidence

Creative thinking

Creative thinking is defined as the process by which we derive a new idea. It is the merging of a series of ideas which have not been combined before. New ideas are made when old ones are joined in our minds. Due to the fact that our brains automatically organize information once it is obtained, we can only think about new ideas in the context of what we already know. Therefore, someone who is constantly acquiring new information will have more of a base of information which with to be creative than someone who remains stagnant in their information acquiring process. Creative thinking is something that can be naturally learned, as every day we come into contact with new information that we can use to create new ideas.

Creative thinking can either be accomplished accidentally, deliberately, or by an ongoing process. When creative thinking is done accidentally, it usually is by a chance encounter where one tries something one might not have tried in a different situation. Through this process, progression can take a long time to develop and improve without any guidance. Deliberate creative thinking can be used to create new ideas from a structure. When certain criteria are provided, these techniques can force a wide range of ideas to develop. For example, students may be given a list of five things to include in a story, from which countless stories could emerge. Finally, ongoing creative thinking is a process that develops through education and self-awareness. It is a process by which seeking improvement never ends. For example, a student working on a short story will have to have a sustained level of creative thinking in order to be able to finish the story successfully.

Bloom's Taxonomy

When developing higher order thinking skills, it is important to use the lower order thinking skills as building blocks. The lower thinking skills in Bloom's Taxonomy are knowledge, comprehension and application. These skills are more focused on observations and ability to summarize ideas learned. They reinforce simple ideas, and are necessary to make sure that a basic understanding of a topic has been reached. But in order to progress to the higher thinking skills, (analysis, synthesis and evaluation), the ability to see things figuratively, instead of literally, becomes important. Bloom's Taxonomy provides teachers with starting words for questions in order to ensure that students

are being challenged at all levels, which caters to multiple intelligences, as well as making sure that students are attempting a variety of work.

Levels of Bloom's Taxonomy

1. Knowledge: This level tests previously learned material and may involved a wide range of materials. It relies heavily on memorization as all it requires is the appropriate information. Terms: list, define, tell, describe, identify, show, label, collect, examine, tabulate, quote, name, who, when and where.
2. Comprehension: This level assesses the ability to grasp the meaning of the material learned that may be shown by interpretation and predication. Terms: summarize, describe, interpret, contrast, predict, associate, distinguish, estimate, differentiate, discuss and extend.
3. Application: This is the ability to use learned information in new situations. This may be shown in the application of rules, concepts and theories. Terms: apply, demonstrate, calculate, complete, illustrate, show, solve, examine, modify, relate, change, classify, experiment and discover.
4. Analysis: This level represents the ability to break down material into its parts so that its organization can be looked at. It may include the identification and labeling of its parts, analyzing these parts or recognizing how they are organized. Terms: analyze, separate, order, explain, connect, classify, arrange, divide, compare, select and infer.
5. Synthesis: By putting parts together to form a new whole is the ability of synthesis tested. It may involve making a speech, a

research proposal or identifying a set of abstractions. Terms: combine, modify, rearrange, substitute, plan, create, design, invent, compose, formulate, prepare, generalize and rewrite.

6. Evaluation: This level tests the ability to judge the value of a material for a certain purpose. It may be based on its organization, on internal criteria, or on some external criteria; the relevance of its purpose. Terms: assess, decide, rank, grade, test, measure, recommend, convince, judge, explain, discriminate, support, conclude, compare and summarize.

Higher order thinking

Firstly, it is important to set up a classroom environment that has the materials to do so. By giving students high expectations, nurturing risk-taking, grouping the students in flexible arrangements and accepting diversity, a classroom will have been created in which students feel safe to take risks and stretch their minds. It is also important to make sure that students are taking part in activities where they can communicate with others, have problems that require creative solutions, develop open-ended activities that have more than one right answer and that accommodate multiple intelligences. This way students will feel that they all have something important to contribute. The final way to incorporate higher order of thinking is to allow yourself to ask students questions to which you may not know the answer and to use a variety of assessments that will challenge all students.

Cognitive learning

Cognitive approaches to learning focus on emphasizing ways to enhance students' intrinsic nature to make sense of the world around them. Students do this by learning and organizing information, problem-solving and finally developing the concepts and language in order to convey what they see. It refers to the way that students process information. The style in which one learns is described as a dimension of one's personality. Attitudes, values, and social interactions are all dimensions of these influences. Once a teacher has an idea of the cognitive learning styles of his students, he can better gauge how to direct the information at them. He may find that one of his classes does much better with small group work, whereas another group works more effectively individually. There will always be a wide range of ability in any class, and getting to know the students' styles is always going to be effective.

Discovery learning theory of Bruner and Piaget

Discovery learning is defined as the process by which learning occurs through one's own efforts. In the classroom, this type of learning happens mostly through structured activities set by the teacher that require students to discover important relationships between ideas or concepts by manipulation, investigation and exploration. This requires higher-order thinking because students are provided with the minimum amount of information and then are required to formulate their own ideas for themselves. For example, students may be given a variety of objects and told to build the tallest structure, and the students must use the previous knowledge of construction to build this new object, eventually arriving at their own conclusion about what works best.

Constructivism

Constructivism is defined as a meaningful learning experience that occurs when

- 18 -

students construct and apply their own meaning to knowledge based on their own subjective experiences and background knowledge of a topic. What is specifically challenging about constructivism is getting students to realize that they all bring preconceptions and misconceptions to the process and how to teach them to avoid doing this when it is inappropriate. By using this in the classroom, students are given the chance to participate in real-life experiences, build self-esteem by referring to previous, successful experiences, and build new thoughts through the questions asked. It is discovery-based learning and aims to make learning relevant to students and invites them to apply their previous experiences.

Ausubel's idea of reception learning

This form of learning requires the ability to receive and process structured information as received by the teacher. In order for this to effective, teacher presentations should be organized from general to specific and should use a variety of organizational tools. This could include introductory information to give students an idea of what will be studied, descriptions of key terms and concepts they will need to know in order to progress, and a certain amount of synthesis between new material and what has already been taught. By referring to previously learned material, students will be able to see how the ideas have progressed, and have the chance to revisit older material that they might have either forgotten or not fully understood the first time it was presented.

Using inquiry based learning in conjunction with other scientific educational learning theories

Inquiry based learning can be used alongside many other educational learning theories. It is a part of multiple intelligence work because it reinforces the fact that all students learn differently and provides them with opportunities to learn in the best way for them. Cooperative learning can also be used in conjunction with it as it sometimes relies on working with groups or pairs and fostering a positive rapport amongst group members in order for everyone to succeed. Finally, using inquiry method is also a key tool for how learning occurs in constructivism because the personal experiences are a part of how we construct our idea of the world around us. New experiences may cause us to change our mental rules and our preconceived notions may be altered.

Assessment, Instruction, and the Learning Environment

Choosing course content and material

Texts and reading should be chosen with gender-neutral language, free of stereotypes. Texts that do include these should be addressed and discussed. The curriculum should be inclusive by including the perspectives and experiences of a pluralistic society. All points of view should be presented so that no one view takes precedence over the others. When making references to culture or history, make sure that your students are given background information and the opportunity to ask for clarification. Do not assume that all of your students will be able to pick up on these references. Considering students needs when assigning homework is also considerate based on the different family structures at home. If requiring the use of a computer, make sure that opportunities to use computers at school are permitted in the case of students who do not have access to one at home.

Encouraging exploration

Exploration is a valuable skill to encourage in the classroom because it will often lead to higher levels of productivity and satisfaction with work, as students will have had more influence on the results. As long as exploration is encouraged regardless of the result, students will feel comfortable trying new things. Students should feel safe as they are experimenting. Constantly trying to guide their behavior, which a teacher may see as being helpful, could restrict their work because most of the time what students come up with will be much

different than what the teacher foresaw. Praising small advances is also important because if the teacher acts disappointed as students try and fail, they will be less willing to try new tasks. Having the task to be completed broken up into small, doable tasks is a better way to encourage success.

Gender-neutral language

Gender neutral language is language that attempts to not refer to either a male or female when coming up with an example where the sex of the person involved cannot be determined. For example, when teaching occupations, make sure that all occupations are either male or female, depending on the word chosen, like chair instead of chairman. It is preferable to avoid regendering terms, therefore chair is preferable to chairwoman if the person being referred to is a woman. Also, avoiding terms that have –ette and –ess endings are good because those tend to be derogatory.

Cultural differences

The cultural differences that might affect behavior include: eye contact, hand movements, silence, religious belief and loss of face. It is important to know the differences that some students may have with eye contact; for example, in some cultures, looking down is seen as a sign of disrespect, whereas with some students that is the way to show respect and that they are paying attention. Some students may laugh or smile out of nervousness when under pressure, falsely leading teachers to assume that they are being rude or misbehaving. Silence is one that varies between genders and cultures. Girls tend to be quieter, and students who are silent when called upon could actually be waiting for more direction instead of the impression that they are not paying attention. Religious beliefs come into effect when doing particular activities that certain religions would find inappropriate, therefore causing students to be reluctant to participate, not because they don't know what to do but because they cannot do the activity.

Probing questions

Prompts used during interviews assist respondents in answering the interview questions. For example, when asked what he liked about being a health educator, a respondent said, "I like feeling like I help people." The interviewer used the follow-up probing question, "How do you think you have helped people as a health educator?" to get a more specific response. It is possible to get someone to look at something in a different way than before.

Effective communication

Repeating key terms or concepts frequently is preferential. The more often students hear something, the more likely they will be to remember it later. Thus, reviewing key concepts often is going to be most effective. Providing students with visual aids to reinforce and explain abstract concepts is going to be more important as today's students tend to be visual learners. Encourage students to use logical thinking when necessary by pointing out which information is fact and which exists logically. This will help students apply knowledge in new situations more readily. By using in-class activities to reinforce newly presented materials, one will allow students to show what they have learned. Having students give feedback about what they have learned will also increase their understanding.

Assist students by creating a link when you are teaching something new. If students can see how it relates to something that they have previously been taught, then the odds of learning the new

material are increased. Vocabulary is something to be considered, both what the teacher uses and what the students use. It should be introduced with a real-life definition and with many opportunities for the students to use the words. Students should be communicated with respectfully and addressed appropriately for the setting in order for them to reciprocate respect. Finally, communicating that students are held to high standards right from the start will let them know what is to be expected and for them to keep striving for their best.

Nonverbal communication

Nonverbal communication is the set of ways in which humans send and receive messages without using words. For teachers, it is just as important to be effective nonverbal communicators as verbal communicators. They are essential aspects of the teaching process and can sometimes even be more effective than a verbal reminder. Nonverbal communication includes gestures, facial expressions, proximity, humor, posture, body orientation or touching. Being aware of the ways the students communicate nonverbally can also assist teachers in getting messages about how their students are learning. Sometimes sending signals can reinforce learning more effectively, because they are implicit and students will learn how to react to your nonverbal communication more readily because it tends to be less confrontational than direct statements.

Four commonly used types of nonverbal communication are eye contact, facial expressions, gestures, and body orientation. Eye contact helps to regulate the flow of communication between two people as well as registering interest in the topic at hand. Teachers who use eye contact convey warmth, concern and directness. Facial expressions are nonverbal communicators that have been taught to us since birth to convey a wide range of emotions. For instance, smiling conveys happiness, warmth, friendless and liking. If teachers smile often, then students will tend to react positively and develop a better feeling toward the class and sometimes even learn more effectively. Gestures can include movements with hands that sometimes serve no larger purpose than entertainment or to keep attention, but can also help an instructor illustrate valuable concepts. Body orientation conveys the message that you are either interested or disinterested in the person speaking to you; leaning forward is more favorable of a position than reclining back in ones chair.

Three other aspects of nonverbal communication include proximity, paralinguistics and humor. Proximity is usually set out by the cultural norms regarding space. When a student is not focusing, sometimes standing next to his desk is just as effective as verbally reminding him to pay attention. Usually having the teacher walk around the room increases interaction with the students. Paralinguistics are the vocal elements of nonverbal communication, such as tone, pitch, rhythm, loudness and inflection. Teachers who speak in a monotone voice tend to be perceived as boring because there is no variety. But, when teachers use variety in their voice, it tends to keep the interest of the students longer. Humor can also be a useful teaching tool because it can release stress and tension for both the teacher and students. It can foster a friendly classroom environment that facilitates learning, and as long as it is used appropriately, is very useful and effective.

Effective communication techniques

Two main ways to ensure generally effective communication techniques involve listening actively and controlling the nonverbal message that is being sent to the speaker. When listening, remain attentive and concentrate on what is being said. Also, don't form an opinion right away; be impartial in order to take the most away from what is being said. Reflecting on that which is being said can be done by restating the message so that the speaker knows that you understand. Summarizing what the speaker has said will also show that you have paid attention to the details. The nonverbal message conveyed is also important. You should be aware of your body posture and the level of eye contact you are using. Staring students directly in the eye could be seen as confrontational, whereas complete lack of eye contact can be viewed as disinterest. If you are speaking to a student, try to have a parallel body position, either both be standing or sitting in order to put you both on an equal level.

Divergent thinking

Divergent thinking is generating many ideas about a topic in a short period of time. It stems from the idea that there is not one right idea, but that many ideas are possible. It involves taking one topic and breaking it down into many smaller parts in order to gain insight about the topic as a whole. Divergent thinking usually occurs in spontaneous, free-flowing ways because the ideas that create this type of thinking often are thought of in these patterns as well. The ideas may then be put back together in a more structured way in order to be understandable to the other students. It can be an effective way for students to start a new topic, as divergent thinking will allow them to examine what they already know about the topic.

Two ways to stimulate divergent thinking are brainstorming and keeping a journal. Brainstorming involves making a list of ideas in a creative, yet unstructured way.

Its goal is to generate as many ideas as possible in a short period of time. It often relies on one idea to spawn the process of thinking in a variety of directions. During brainstorming, all ideas are seen as important and no idea is disregarded or criticized. They are all seen as important because of the thought process. After brainstorming is complete, only then can the list be reviewed and the best ideas sorted out from the rest. Keeping a journal is also an effective way to record ideas on a daily basis. It can take the form of a small notebook, or just a piece of paper on which to jot ideas. This is useful because students sometimes will gather inspiration at unusual times and places, and by always having a journal handy, it can be ensured that the ideas do not go to waste.

Free writing and mind- or subject-mapping are two others ways that can stimulate divergent thinking. Free writing is when a student focuses on one particular topic and writes non-stop about it for a short period of time. It could be on an idea that was spawned during brainstorming, or on a new unit in a class. It is useful to generate a variety of thought on a topic that can then be used for later work in the unit once it is restructured or put into a logical order. Finally, mind- or subject-mapping involves taking all the brainstormed ideas and putting them into a visual organizer that shows the relationship between the ideas. It may start with a central theme, and then show all the topics related to the theme and their subtopics.

Convergent thinking

Convergent thinking is that which represents the analysis or integration of already taught or previous knowledge. It leads one to an expected end result or answer. It usually involves the terms explaining, stating relationships, and comparing and contrasting. The way it is structured may differ, but the expected result will be a justified answer to the topic. Questions to rouse convergent thinking usually begin with why, how or in what ways. These ensure that the thinking is led in a certain direction with the answer always in mind. Using these question tags effectively will require specific events or people so that the students know what the expected answer should involve.

Motivation

Motivation is defined as the selection, direction and continuation of behavior. Some teachers believe that some students are unmotivated, which is not a correct statement. As long as each student is able to set goals for himself and able to achieve them, then he will not be unmotivated. What is usually meant by this is that students are not motivated to behave in the way teachers would like them to behave. Another misconception is that one person, usually a teacher, can directly motivate another person or a student. This is also inaccurate because motivation comes from within the student. Teachers need to be able to use all kinds of motivation theories in their classroom in order to be able to find that which motivates all of their students. The more ideas students are exposed to, the easier this will be able to happen.

Second language acquisition

Stage 1: Pre-production: Most English language learners (ELL) will have a limited range of English words but will not speak voluntarily. They may repeat what you say to them, and be able to copy from the board. Observing body language is important at this stage in order to judge the student's progress when it cannot be done through language.

Stage 2: Early production: This stage will last for about six months in which the student will learn to speak in one or two word phrases. They can use memorized sentences although they might not be used correctly. Assigning a language buddy at these two stages will be helpful. Remember, however, that for these students, it is exhaustive to be attempting to learn a new language for an entire school day, so progress may be slow to appear.

Helping new English language learners (ELL) in the classroom

It may be helpful to introduce aspects of the ELL student's culture and language to the other students in order to have a smooth transition. Then other students may approach the ELL student in order for them to build up confidence talking to peers, which will often happen before they feel comfortable talking to adults. It is also helpful to ask clear cut yes or no questions and not expect more than yes or no answers. Depending on the language, having a dictionary of their language in the classroom may be helpful if the student does not bring one themselves. The student should have the chance to participate in whole class activities. Using pictures to increase vocabulary is also an effective way to convey ideas to ELL students and can help their spelling and reading skills as well.

How gender differences work differently in the classroom

Many observational studies have found that girls are treated differently than boys in the classroom setting; more often to the girls' detriment. This is primarily because males tend to have more interaction with the teachers as their behavior is more assertive and they tend to dominate class discussions, whereas females tend to sit quietly and be passive. Boys tend to call out and are encouraged to participate, but when girls call out, their behavior is corrected and they are more likely to be called on if they raise their hands. Teachers also exhibit lower expectations for girls in classes such as math and science. Despite these issues, girls are tending to do better in school overall, except mainly in issues of self-esteem, of which boys tend to have much higher levels when high school is completed.

Inequities between how girls and boys are treated in their classrooms

1. Being metacognitive of the way they deal with girls and boys differently
2. Ensuring that boys and girls are not segregating themselves in the classroom by having a mixed seating plan. Having a seating plan that alternates boy-girl-boy-girl can also be an effective classroom management tool.
3. Checking resources, such as textbooks and videos, to make sure that both sexes are represented equally in a variety of roles. If there is a textbook or video that has a gender bias, it can be used to spark a conversation on the topic.
4. Planning activities so that both sexes have an equal opportunity to participate, such as rewarding those students who raise their hands before calling out.
5. Having a classroom culture, and more importantly, a school culture, that does not tolerate gender bias.

Mainstreaming

Traditional mainstreaming in public schools is defined as allowing students with physical disabilities to be placed in certain regular education classes. As practiced in the 1970s and early '80s, mainstreaming was an attempt to meet the LRE requirement by moving students from separate schools and classes into regular education classes for part or all of the school day. Often, students received their academic instruction in special classes and their time with nondisabled peers was spent in nonacademic activities such as lunch, recess, physical education, or perhaps art and music. This seems to be an easy thing to do, but the fact is that in order for this to be effective and beneficial for all the students involved, there must be the correct support services in place. Otherwise, the classroom teacher may be spread too thin if she is expected to differentiate for the student with the disability on her own. Due to this some schools will only mainstream children with mild to moderate disabilities, instead of all students with disabilities. If a school is fully committed to the idea of mainstreaming students with disabilities, it should be done so with support in the regular classroom in order to make the transition run smoothly.

Inclusion

Inclusion is defined as the commitment to educate the child, to the highest possible effect, in a regular school and classroom. It outlines bringing the support to the students in the classroom, such as special supplies, or other teachers, rather than separating them in separate rooms or buildings altogether. People who support inclusion could argue that students with disabilities who are educated separately are being discriminated against and therefore it violates their rights. They also voice a need for reform in the special education programs, which they argue are costly for the often inadequate results that they produce, both academically and socially. However, some special educators and teachers have voiced their concerns that inclusion could result in insufficient services for students with disabilities. A regular classroom may not be the place for children with behavioral problems or anti-social disorders. There is also the concern that inclusion could replace special education altogether one day.

Inclusion vs. mainstreaming

The traditional idea of mainstreaming allows students with disabilities to participate in some regular classrooms whereas inclusion allows these same students the ability to participate in all regular classrooms and activities. Generally, inclusion is thought of as the better option to better avoid the segregation that can sometime occur between students with disabilities and without. If they are mainstreamed, they are only mainstreamed in certain classes, whereas with inclusion, more possibilities are open to them, and depending on what is outlined in their IEP, they may have one-on-one support in the classrooms they are in. It also gives them the opportunity to participate in the same activities that all students participate in to the greatest extent possible, thus following the order that all students with disabilities be educated in the least restrictive environment possible.

Effects of mainstreaming on academic and social performance

Mainstreaming, when done correctly, can have many positive effects on social performance. If the students in the regular classroom are educated about the students with disabilities that could be entering their classrooms, then the rate of success tends to be much higher. If no transition work is done, then isolation can be the result, which is the exact opposite of the goal of mainstreaming. For academic performance, as long as the right support systems are in place in the regular classroom (such as a paraeducator and any necessary adaptations to the assigned work), then the academic performance of students

- 25 -

with disabilities can only improve. Mainstreaming is meant to increase awareness and to welcome diversity, and when done properly, a classroom is a great place in which for this change to occur.

Dealing with the different needs of students with disabilities

The most important thing to remember is to not stereotype students solely because of their appearance. A student in a wheelchair does not automatically have a learning disability, merely because his physical disability is more apparent, whereas a student with mental retardation may require repetition in order to master the most simple of tasks. Students with disabilities may be in your classroom for varying amounts of time during the day. Making use of the special education staff in your school to familiarize yourselves with the abilities of your students will enable you to assist them to the best of their abilities in your classroom. Ultimately, they are treated as you would treat any student. You need to assess their abilities, finding their strengths and weaknesses, and use your resources to provide the best classroom learning experience for them.

Individualized Education Program (IEP)

IDEA sets out the steps to ensure that each student with a disability has access to a fair and equal education. One component of this is that each student diagnosed with a disability should have an IEP, which is a written statement made in conjunction with the student, parents/guardians, school officials and teachers. It must include an analysis of the student's present achievement level, outline goals, both long-term and short term, as well as describe the steps to be taken to assist the student in achieving these goals. It should also specify the extent to which the student will be able to participate in regular education programs. It should be clear about the length and duration of these services and gives the details of how this program will be checked for any necessary revisions and the progress achieved.

In the creation of an IEP, there can be disputes as to what is best for each student, and due process protects the rights of parents to have their voices heard in this process. If parents and school officials disagree with one another, an impartial hearing may take place for mediation, where both sides meet with an impartial person who helps them find terms upon which both can agree upon. There also may be an impartial due process hearing between both parties who present their cases and a hearing officer decides what is appropriate based on the law requirements. All parents should receive an outline of special education procedures which describes the steps for due process hearings and mediation.

Special education teachers help to develop an Individualized Education Program (IEP) for each special education student. The IEP sets personalized goals for each student and is tailored to the student's individual needs and ability. When appropriate, the program includes a transition plan outlining specific steps to prepare students with disabilities for middle school or high school or, in the case of older students, a job or postsecondary study. Teachers review the IEP with the student's parents, school administrators, and the student's general education teacher. Teachers work closely with parents to inform them of their child's progress and suggest techniques to promote learning at home.

Outline how to differentiate the content of a task in the classroom setting

Differentiating the content requires that students are pre-tested in some degree so that the teacher can tell which students do not require direct instruction and instead can do some independently guided learning. This would occur if perhaps some students already understand the concept and can begin applying the concept to solve a problem. Another way of doing this is simply to have able students accelerate their rate of progress by outlining their own course of action for the task. This will allow the teacher enough time to go over the content of a task in enough detail that other students will be able to understand it thoroughly before moving on to the next step.

Classroom assignment

To have differentiation in the process of a task means that students need a variety of learning activities and strategies in order to be able to explore the concepts in the best way possible. They need to be made aware of all the possible ways to manipulate and consider the ideas in the concept. Some ways of assisting this would be graphic organizers, charts, graphs or diagrams in order to display their understanding of the material covered. By varying the required complexity of the graphic organizer, this allows for each student to be challenged according to their ability. This would work well in a classroom with a wide variety of students because it is most independently guided work.

Assessment strategies

An assessment is an illustrative task or opportunity to perform that targets the educational objectives for an assignment and allows students to demonstrate what they have learned and the progress of their learning. There are many strategies that can be used as strategies to assess student learning. Graphic organizers can allow the presentation of a variety of information or show how the information was obtained and learned. Interviewing others can provide a real life experience to a topic studied in class and put a face to the story and experience. Doing an observation can help students see how the topic appears in real life. If students complete self or peer evaluations, these can be useful because sometimes feedback from a peer group is more valuable than that of a teacher. Finally, portfolios can contain a little bit of everything and can track how the students have progressed through the assessment.

Assessment rubrics

Assessment rubrics are authentic assessment tools that are used to measure the work of students. It aims to evaluate a student's performance based on a set of criteria related to the task, rather than giving a single score for the work. Students usually receive the rubric before they attempt the task so that they know what is expected and for them to think about how the criteria will play out in their work. They can be analytic or holistic and are tailored to individual assessment tasks, allowing teachers to design the rubric for individual classes and the needs of the students. Rubrics are also a formative type of assessment because it is an ongoing part of the teaching and learning process since it is revealed to the students before the assessment is even commenced.

Performance-based assessment

Performance-based assessments are concerned with problem solving and understanding. The goal of this type of assessment is that students should be able to show their understanding of a topic studied that falls in line with certain curriculum goals. These types of assessment can provide a measure of achievement as well as track a teacher's progress with an individual student. They could take the form of essays, oral presentations, open-ended problems, role-playing or hands-on tasks. It could also take the form of a portfolio that students put together throughout the study of a certain topic that shows how their learning has taken place over a period of study. Self-evaluation also has a place in performance-based assessment as the students often have to be critical of themselves and the process it took them to get to the finished result.

Quantitative measurement

A quantitative measurement uses results from an instrument based on a standardized system that limits the collection of data to a preset amount of possible responses. This is more commonly known as a standardized test, such as the ACT or SAT to get into college, or any test with multiple choice responses. This type of measurement is more concerned with the details of performance and can be used as both a pre-and post-subject assessment of performance after knowledge on a certain topic has been studied. When these tests are given in the classroom, they can be more effective if a more experienced teacher has created the test in order to ensure that concepts are being tested, not just facts and ideas.

Quantitative measurement vs. performance-based assessment

Both types of assessment have their place in the classroom, as long as they are used accurately. It would not be useful, for example, to have a multiple-choice test after having students read a book in order to show their interpretation of a book. It

would, however, be appropriate to have a standardized test regarding vocabulary or the background to a novel, to then be taken after the text to see how much the students have learned. Performance-based assessment tends to be more individually driven by each student and by that fact alone it tends to be a more exciting form of assessment. However, it requires a lot of thought on the teacher's part in order to make sure that all the choices are relevant to the topic and can be graded on some sort of scale.

Alternative means of assessment

By having a variety of products that the students can produce, they will be more likely to choose something that catches their interest, therefore having some intrinsic motivation to do well at the task. The product can be varied in complexity depending upon what ability level upon which each student is working. Students who are working below grade level may have the performance expectations reduced, whereas students who are working above grade level may be asked to demonstrate higher and more complex learning processes in their adaptation of the product. By giving the students the choice of what they are working on, a natural differentiation occurs because each student will automatically adjust the task to his ability level.

Assessment of students with dual exceptionalities

Identification of giftedness in students who are disabled is problematic. The customary identification methods (i.e., standardized tests and observational checklists) are inadequate without major modification. Standard lists of characteristics of gifted students may be inadequate for unmasking hidden potential in children who have disabilities. Children whose hearing is impaired, for example, cannot respond to oral directions, and they may also lack the vocabulary which reflects the complexity of their thoughts. Children whose speech or language is impaired cannot respond to tests requiring verbal responses. Children whose vision is impaired may be unable to respond to certain performance measures, and although their vocabulary may be quite advanced, they may not understand the full meaning of the words they use (e.g., color words). Children with learning disabilities may use high-level vocabulary in speaking but be unable to express themselves in writing, or vice versa. In addition, limited life experiences due to impaired mobility may artificially lower scores. Because the population of gifted/disabled students is difficult to locate, they are seldom included in standardized test norming groups, adding to the problems of comparison. In addition, gifted children with disabilities often use their intelligence to try to circumvent the disability. This may cause both exceptionalities to appear less extreme; using one to mask the other normalizes both.

Standard error of measurement

Standard error of measurement is the estimate of the 'error' associated with the test-taker's obtained score when compared with their hypothetical 'true' score. The SEM, which varies from test to test, should be given in the test manual. The band of scores in which we can be fairly certain the 'true' score lies can be calculated from this figure.

Raw score and scaled score

Raw score is an original datum that has not been transformed. A standard score is a dimensionless quantity derived from the raw score.

Scaled score is a standardized score, that is, it is based upon the normal distribution and standard deviation units.

Mastery level

Mastery levels are the cutoff score on a criterion-referenced or mastery test; people who score at or above the cutoff score are considered to have mastered the material; mastery may be an arbitrary judgment.

Syncretism

Syncretism is the conscious adopting of the cultural elements of a dominant group by a subordinate group. One classic example of this kind of syncretism is the economic transformation of Japan after World War Two. The Japanese, with help from the Western powers, rapidly developed an industrial base and market economy modeled after that of the United States. Syncretism has often been used to describe the interplay of religions within a society; for example, it is invoked hopefully by those who would like to see reconciliation between the Protestant and Catholic churches. Sociologists note that there is a danger in syncretism of losing elements of culture that are unique to the subordinate culture, and thus discouraging debate and innovation.

Standard deviation

Standard Deviation is a measure of the range of values in a set of numbers. Standard deviation is a statistic used as a measure of the dispersion or variation in a distribution, equal to the square root of the arithmetic mean of the squares of the deviations from the arithmetic mean. The standard deviation of a random variable or list of numbers (the lowercase Greek sigma) is the square root of the variance. The standard deviation of the list [x1, x2, x3] with a mean value of 5 is given by the formula:

$$\sigma = \sqrt{\frac{(x1-5)^2 + (x2-5)^2 + (x3-5)^2}{3}}$$

In this formula, sigma (the standard deviation) is equal to the square root of the variance, which is given as the sum of each value minus the mean, squared, divided by the total number of values. This formula is used when all of the values in the population are known. If the values x1...xn are a random sample chosen from the population, then the sample Standard Deviation is calculated with same formula, except that (n-1) is used as the denominator.

Grade equivalent score

What the grade equivalent score actually measures is how typical students at the grade level specified would perform on the test that has been given. In other words, a 4th grader's grade equivalent of 10.4 does not indicate that the 4th grade is capable of doing 10th grade work. Rather, it indicates that the 4th grade student has performed as well as a typical 10th grade student would have performed on the 4th grade test. If the student is performing on grade level, that is a 4th grade student taking the test in the 10th month of 4th grade receives a score of 4.10, then it simply indicates that he/she is performing right at the average for other 4th graders in the norming sample, which is the 50th percentile and 50th NCE. Grade equivalents do not lend themselves to measuring aggregate performance of all students in a school or school district, nor do they average well and are hard to understand when dealing with groups. Accordingly, the score used more often is the Normal Curve Equivalent, or NCE.

Testing modifications

Directions
Key words could be underlined by the teacher, or the teacher could read the directions aloud and ask if there are any questions before beginning.

Adapted Expectations
The grading scale could be altered to account for students with lower cognitive functioning that may know some of the concepts, but not all of them.

Time constraints
Extended test time with supervision could be determined to be appropriate depending on the student and his IEP.

Essay questions
Completing an outline could be an option, or having the student verbalize answers onto a tape recorder, or having someone else transcribe his answers.

Additional tools
For some tests, formulas, sample problems, dictionaries or computers may be used in order to facilitate the test-taking process.

School culture

The culture of a school is defined as the set of norms, values, beliefs, symbols and rituals that make up the school. These are built up over time as the parents, teachers, parents and students work together in order to solve problems. Schools also have rituals that take place in order to build up a sense of school community, such as assemblies, plays, or sporting events. It can also be conveyed by the atmosphere of the school and the appearance of the staff and students. How the staff functions together and with the administrators is also important to see whether it is positive or negative. If student groups are able to meet readily with teachers and administrators and be able to collaborate in problem solving, then this usually provides a good pathway in order to have a positive environment between the students and the adults in the building.

Bilingual education

There are three main types of bilingual education: the submersion model, where the students are dropped into all-English classes and must learn English or fail; the immersion model, where students are taught by a teacher who understands their language but only speaks in English to them; and the transitional model, where the child's native tongue is used only to transition and explain English to them until they achieve fluency. Other lesser used types of bilingual education include maintenance and ESL, where there is a mix of instruction in the native language, and teachers who do not know their native language who teach the basics of the English language until fluency is enough to attend regular English classes more often.

Controversy that surrounds bilingual education

With an influx of Spanish speakers, many states have hurried English-only legislation that makes English the official language of the state. Some groups assert that bilingual education actually impedes the English skills of minorities since they are receiving their education primarily in their native language. Some would also argue that English is the language of the U.S. and that students should study the language of the country in which they live. However, there are many benefits to bilingual education, and many studies have proven that children who have the knowledge of two or more languages tend to achieve higher academically than those students who only know their native language. Certain bilingual programs have proven to be more effective than

others, such as immersion programs or programs gradually including English instruction over a period of time.

Classroom reward structures

Competitive goal structures: Grading that is done on a curve only allows a certain number of students to achieve at any one level, therefore any accomplishment comes at another student's expense. Students constantly feel the need to outdo one another, even focusing on each other's failures to try to get ahead. It can cause students to believe that achievement is ability based, and if they don't believe they have the ability to succeed, then they will never try to do so.

Individual goal structures: Students work alone and earn rewards based on their individual performance. They do not concern themselves with the efforts of other students.

Cooperative goal structures: Students work together to achieve shared goals. Since the group can only achieve well if all its members work together, then positive interdependence is important to the group.

Motivating students to learn

1. Ensure that students know what they are doing and how to know when they have achieved a goal in order for them to build their self-esteem and self-awareness.
2. Do everything possible to satisfy the basic needs of the students, such as esteem, safety and belongingness.
3. Try to encourage students to take risks in order to grow by talking up the rewards.
4. Direct learning experiences toward feelings of success, in order to direct students towards

individual and group achievement.

5. Encourage the development of self-confidence and self-direction in students who needed help working on these qualities.
6. Make learning relevant for the students by focusing on social interaction, usefulness and activity.

Major developers in classroom management theories

Lee and Marlene Canter
They viewed classroom management as establishing and enforcing classroom rules as a way of controlling student behavior, mainly by discipline.

Carl Rogers
Socioemotional climate was given importance by Rogers because he thought that having positive interpersonal relationship between students and teachers would foster a positive classroom.

Richard and Patricia Schmuck
They derived group process from social psychology and group dynamics research and put the emphasis on the teacher establishing and maintaining an effectively controlled classroom with cooperation being the key skills needed in order to have groups work effectively together.

B.F. Skinner
He outlined behavior modification which originated from behavioral psychology. He thought that the best way to change students' behavior was to reward them for good behavior and remove rewards, or punish, inappropriate behavior.

Biggest concern for new teachers

Classroom management is defined as the set of rules or activities that the teacher sets for his classroom that outline effective and efficient instruction. This can range from establishing attendance and homework routines to dealing with inappropriate behavior. Some would argue that classroom management cannot be taught and that it is something that can only be learned through experience. Nonetheless, it doesn't do anyone any good to have a new teacher in a classroom with no idea of good ways to instill order in his classroom. Being organized is the first way to start off with a good classroom management program, as well as having an experienced teacher as a mentor, are usually good ways for a new teacher to overcome his fears about classroom management as he will have someone to whom to turn for help.

Daily procedures, routines and rules

The most important thing to remember when dealing with students is that consistency is vital. If one student sees you deal with something in a certain way, the next student will expect the same treatment. If she is treated differently, then she will see your rules as flexible, or that they don't even matter. It is better to be tough at the beginning of the school year, and as many teachers will tell you— "Don't smile until after Christmas"—you are ultimately there in the classroom to be a teacher, not a friend to the students, and remaining firm with your rules and routines will earn their respect as well as maintain an orderly classroom. Empty threats can be especially damaging. It is best to clearly outline the consequences for misbehavior, or inability to produce class work or homework as soon as possible and then follow through.

Choosing relevant consequences

When deciding on rewards and consequences, it is useful to make sure that they are relevant to the students and the situation. It makes sense to punish a

- 32 -

student who does not complete his homework by having them complete the homework in a detention after school, or having the student complete it by a certain date, otherwise the parents would be notified. It would not be appropriate, for example, to have the student stand in the hallway, when he could be in the class learning the material. When students see clear links between the consequences and their behavior, they will know their limits and be more inclined to behave appropriately or complete assignments on time.

Positive guidance

When the differences between girls and boys were looked at in many gender studies, it was found that boys tended to be more assertive and aggressive, while the girls tended to be passive. The way the teachers were dealing with the boys tended to be more verbal, thus reinforcing that calling out would get more attention than the more desirable behavior of the girls who would raise their hands and pay attention. Praising and giving compliments encourages students to focus and stay on task if they want to receive praise and attention. Ignoring misbehavior can be effective, as long as it doesn't get out of hand, at ensuring that the misbehaving students know that negative behavior will get a negative reaction, or no reaction at all. Focusing on the problems in a classroom can inadvertently be rewarding to those who misbehave and cause the negative behavior to manifest itself further.

Successful classroom management

Positive classroom environment
Developing a friendly rapport with students from the first day onwards so that students will feel eager to come to class is important. Criticism of work should be worded by what the student has done well, and then some suggestions as to how to improve it, focusing on the positive aspects first.

Clear standards of behavior for students
Rules should be enforced consistently so that there is no surprise as to what students should expect for misbehaving. Dealing with inappropriate behaviors should be done so with a calm and clear demeanor.
Student engagement: Having students engaged in the task will help with classroom management as there should be less inappropriate behaviors. Smooth transitions are also important so that there is no time in between activities for students to lose their concentration.

Daily classroom management success

Ensure that students know the routines; always over plan for lessons; label materials clearly so that they do not need much further explanation; make sure expectations are clearly set for your students; discussions, debates and consequences are more effective than nagging, lecturing and threatening; review rules for behavior and work periodically; welcome students at the door; make sure there is plenty of opportunity for student participation; learn about the students' interests; involve students who misbehave; assign work ahead of time and give clear deadlines; color code materials in order to help organization; use eye contact; use both verbal and non-verbal ways to correct behavior; use humor daily; give your students compliments when they deserve them.

Classroom rule system

Starting off the school year with a clearly defined set of classroom rules will let your students know their limitations from the beginning. Many teachers have their students participate in the creation of the rules. Starting off by brainstorming ideas

- 33 -

for rules may have you discover that student-created rules may be more strict than rules you would create yourself. Most students want to learn in a safe environment and feel better when there are defined boundaries. It is useful to create consequences after each repetition of the undesirable; for example, after the first violation, the student's name goes on the board. After the second violation, the student stands in the hallway, and after the third violation there is a note home, detention or whatever the relevant consequence may be.

Creating classroom rules

The rules should be positive by nature. Some students tend to see rules that are worded negatively as a challenge and will attempt to break the rule, for example, "Raise your hand before speaking," is worded positively, whereas: "Don't call out," is worded negatively. Rules should also be worded as simply as possible, but should be well-defined in a discussion before it is decided upon. For example, if "Be respectful to others" is one of your rules, make sure the students know what respecting someone looks like by providing examples. Keeping the list short is also important because students will be more likely to keep to them if there are just a few. And lastly, enforce the rules that are created. It does no good for the students to see a rule being broken by another student who does not receive the prescribed consequences.

Natural consequences

Natural consequences are results of behavior that are not planned or controlled but the result of a behavior. For example, if a student is working and another student steals her pen, the first student will probably not lend the other student a pen in the future. Teachers do not have any control over these consequences because they are merely the natural reaction to an undesirable behavior. Teachers can, however, teach students how to predict these behaviors; for example, if a student would like to borrow money from their parents, doing something nice for them will probably cause the parent to look favorably upon their child rather than having their child show them a bad report card and then asking them for money.

Logical consequences do not occur naturally due to a behavior but instead are implemented by teachers. They are similar to the consequences that an adult would face and they therefore teach students what to expect in life and should be related, respectful and reasonable. A related logical consequence means that the consequence has a clear link to the student's behavior. For this one it is important that a teacher knows his students in order to make sure that the consequences are related to each student. For example, having a consequence be an after school detention for not completing homework may be effective for a student in after-school sports, but not for a student who picks up their sisters from elementary school. Consequences need to be given respectfully so that the student understands how her behavior led to being punished. Finally, consequences should be reasonable and understood by the student.

Why students misbehave

Attention
Some students feel that they belong in a classroom only when they are being noticed, whether this be by a teacher or fellow student. Giving positive attention to these students will ensure that they do not resort to negative behavior in order to obtain it.

Inadequacy
When students have a low self-esteem or self-worth, they don't believe that they can succeed at anything and will develop

feelings of inadequacy and misbehave to distract attention from the fact that they struggle at classroom tasks.

Power
Some students want to be in control. It is important to ensure that consequences are clear and followed so that the students do not completely disregard them.

Revenge
There will be some students who will hurt other students. Encouraging students and fostering a safe classroom environment will ensure that no students feel the need to hurt others or themselves.

Consequences vs. punishment

Natural and logical consequences are often confused with punishments. Of course, teachers have wanted inappropriate behaviors of students to be stopped and have used means such as writing sentences, isolation and corporal punishment in the past in order to do so. As a result, the term punishment is negatively viewed because of the types of punishment used in the past. Using natural and logical consequences has been the result of wanting to use noninvasive consequences in order to deal with behavior. Although some would argue that only using these types of "positive" consequences does not represent real life and will leave students ill-prepared for the punishments that do exist for adults. Therefore, the most balanced classroom management policies will teach students that they have to deal with the responsibilities of their actions and are parallel with real-life situations that they may face as adults.

Wasted time

This logical consequence is based on the idea that both the teacher and the students in the classroom have important jobs to do. The main reason why school exists is for learning to take place, and anyone who interferes with that is wasting time. Students should, from the beginning, see the connection between school and what they want to do with their lives. This will help them understand that when they misbehave and suffer the consequences, that it is not from the teacher but it is because of their own action or inaction. If a student is choosing to interfere with someone's job in the classroom, then she is wasting time. The teacher can give her the choice to stop wasting time and let her know that she will make it up. If the student chooses to continue, then she will lose some of her free time later in order to make it up.

Feedback

The main difference that must be outlined when giving feedback is whether the feedback is relating to the students' work or is about the students themselves. Therefore giving feedback that improves the students' self-esteem rather than damaging it is something that must be carefully defined. Some theorists in the past thought that students did better in the face of criticism because they would want to improve on their work and that would be the drive behind improvement. Constant praise was thought to only fuel under-achievement as the students thought they had already received perfection and wouldn't strive to achieve any better. It is not to say that students should never have their behavior corrected or receive any criticism, but the feedback they receive should clearly be a criticism of what the students produced, not of the students themselves.

Helpful and unhelpful feedback

Helpful feedback should: be prompt, occur right after the event, contain encouragement for the student to do even better next time, be specific about what

- 35 -

was positive and negative, and focus clearly on a few aspects rather than a host of different ones. If the teacher can identify the students' weaknesses, then that will help the student correct her own problems, instead of having the teacher do all the work for her. Unhelpful feedback could be: generalized and vague, leaving the student with unclear feelings about what to change; giving an opinion instead of objectively pointing out problems with the work, or focused on an aspect that the student cannot change. The student should be able to hear the respect in any feedback, and in all types of feedback, fact and description should be the focus, not the personal opinion of the teacher.

Communicating effectively with parents

Being able to communicate effectively with parents can be the key to having a successful classroom. If parents feel that you are keeping their interests in mind when you are teaching, it will be that much easier to communicate with them when you have concerns with their children. Having parents support you at home will enforce the idea in the classroom that you are the teacher and there are certain expectations you have of the students. Communicating effectively can mean making phone calls when both positive and negative feedback about their children can be given. It is important to remember that all families have strengths to build upon, most parents really do care about their children, cultural differences are both valid and valuable, different forms of families exist and all are important, and parents have valuable perspectives about their children to share with you.

When face-to-face conferences are not always possible, there are many other ways to communicate with parents, such as phone calls, emails, newsletters, or class websites. With phone calls, try to discuss both positive and negative issues, especially if it's the first phone call to the parents. This will set a precedent for all other calls that you do not only call when there is something negative that happened. It is also important to keep a record of all communications in order to refer to them in subsequent communications. Parents should know how to contact the teacher if there are problems, and they should feel just as comfortable contacting you as you feel about contacting them.

Newsletter or classroom website

Most parents will appreciate communication from the classroom and its daily routines. A classroom website could be helpful if they are computer literate, otherwise a monthly or weekly newsletter could be just as effective. Possibilities for either's content could include: announcements of upcoming events or class trips, reminders about homework or other deadlines with projects, list of items needed for class projects (presentation boards, folders, etc), descriptions of units and ways to continue learning at home, lists of homework assignments or other work students could complete at home for enrichment, explanations of class rules and behavior standards as well as consequences, outlines of grading policies and other assessments, or resources in the community that will complement any work done in the classroom, such as museum exhibits or plays.

Arranging classroom space

Well-run classrooms often begin with the physical layout of the space; how well the desks are arranged and how easily accessible the materials and supplies are to the teacher and the students. The arrangement of your classroom will reflect your teaching style. For example, if you want a lot of small cooperative group work, then make sure that the desks are in small clusters around the room. If you tend to have more large-group discussions, then having the desks in a U-shape so that everyone is visible is the best way to organize the room. However, the most important aspect is making sure that all materials are organized and accessible to you. There should also be a cupboard or shelf with materials that students can access easily to avoid asking you and interrupting the lesson, or waiting in line instead of commencing their work.

Temperature, lighting and noise level are all important environmental features that are a part of your classroom. These three, if controlled properly, can have a large influence on your classroom management. Lighting is important because if it is too bright, it can cause some students to be restless or hyperactive. If possible, having lamps in one area to create a dimly-lit reading area with chairs, plants and cushions could be helpful if the resources are available to you. As for the noise level, have the students demonstrate what good noise levels are by some demonstrations. Temperature is something over which teachers often have no control, but making sure that students dress appropriately is a good way to be proactive.

Problem solving

There are seven steps that can be used in dealing with any problem that the students will face in a classroom. Introducing this to students can encourage them to use their own resources before they ask for help from the teacher. The first step is to identify the problem, then, is to look for possible causes of the problem. Thirdly, coming up with as many ideas as possible for solving the problem leads to the fourth step which is deciding which is the best way to deal with it. Following this, come up with an action plan just in case the solution doesn't work, which you will then do as you are monitoring how the problem solving is going. The last step is to finalize how the problem has been solved and if it has done so clearly.

Cooperative learning

Cooperative learning is using small groups that work together in order to maximize the level of every student's learning process. After receiving instruction from the teacher, small groups are organized and must complete a small task, working through the assignment as a group so that everyone knows what is going on, and then give feedback to the class as a whole or the teacher as required. When cooperative learning is done properly, all members of the group will assist each other so that everyone is able to succeed. It also works off the idea that everyone has something to learn from the other and that everyone has a role in the group. For example, if a group is putting together a PowerPoint presentation on whales, some students will be better at the research aspect, others with the technology, and some with the actual presentation.

Cooperative learning is a strategy that can be used in a classroom to increase the level of positive interdependence among students. It teaches them that everyone has strengths and when these resources are used, that everyone can benefit from them. It does not cause the students to compete against one another, but instead to focus on the positive aspects about everyone, instead of the negative ones that seem to take more importance in a competitive environment. It will also give the students many skills to use in real-life as being able to communicate effectively with others is an important life skill. Cooperative learning can increase levels of self-esteem, lead to higher levels of productivity and achievement, and create a positive classroom environment.

Just because students are assigned to work in groups does not always mean that they will work effectively. As with any other part of learning, students must be taught how to work in groups. For example, having students sit in groups while the teacher is giving a lesson could be met with competition as the students will be more likely to talk and be disruptive. Lessons must be structured cooperatively, with opportunities to work in groups as part of the structure. Choosing groups for the students ahead of time will allow the teacher to tailor the work to each group, once he knows the strengths and weaknesses of each student. It is also important to make sure that the groups are able to accomplish the learning goals set out for them and the class by tailoring the lessons accordingly.

Effective structure of cooperative learning groups

1. Positive interdependence is the most important aspect of cooperative learning. When group members sense that they are reliant on one another for success, they will realize that if they do not cooperate, then they will fail, and if they cooperate, that they will succeed.
2. Having the students interact with each other by doing real work is how they can share resources, support and help each other. By going through the motions together, they will see each other's strengths and weaknesses, and support each other's learning.
3. Individual and group accountability must be instilled so that students will not only feel responsible for their own

contributions to the group, but also encourage others to do so.
4. Students must be equipped with the necessary small group skills before attempting this type of work. It should be introduced in small doses until students know how to work together effectively.

Direct instruction

Direct instruction is defined as the procedure that is led by the teacher and is followed by the students. Students are given specific instructions as to what they are supposed to do. The teacher will introduce the task, providing background information, give the students work to complete individually, and then provide immediate feedback. The two main forms are lecturing and explaining, but could also include a question-answer session or a class discussion. By having the teacher relaying all of the information to the students, and then having the students practice the skills they have just learned, it can be easy to judge how well the students are progressing with the work.

Advantages of direct instruction

Direct instruction can have its advantages. If, for example, the material is simple and there is only one right answer, such as facts, then direct instruction can be the quickest and easiest way to convey this material. The teacher has control of the timing of the lesson and can make sure that it moves at a pace that is accessible to everyone. Also, the teacher has control over what will be learned and how it will be taught, so she can make it relevant to the majority of the students and cater it to the needs of the students to some degree. It is also easier to measure if the curriculum is being taught using this model of instruction because the teacher will be able to progress along a certain line of thought of teaching.

- 38 -

Disadvantages of direct instruction

Some of the disadvantages of direct instruction are that it is based on old theories of learning that believe that simple tasks must be learned before complex ones, and that the emphasis is on learning that can be quantified. This type of instruction can also minimize the prior experiences and knowledge of the individual students as the students are taught as a whole, not as individuals. Sometimes, students can lose sight of the overall task as they are caught up in the series of tasks that can make learning seem irrelevant to them. If students are not given many opportunities to do the work themselves, they can have a low retention level of what they have learned. Finally, students who learn in styles other than verbally may struggle to keep up with the lesson because various learning strategies are not catered to.

Madeline Hunter Direct Instruction Model

1. Anticipatory Set: This should involve the bait for students to show interest in the lesson and for the teacher to focus their attention.
2. Objectives: The objectives should be clear, so that the teacher knows what students will have achieved by the end of the lesson.
3. Teaching: The teacher provides the information, and then shows examples of the material.
4. Guided practice: Students demonstrate what they have learned through an activity supervised by the teacher.
5. Checking for Understanding: The teacher may ask students questions to check understanding in order to proceed to the next level of learning.
6. Independent practice: Once students have mastered the skills, more practice can be done for reinforcement.
7. Closure: The teacher gives the lesson a conclusion and gives the students a chance to make sense of what they have learned.

Discovery learning

Discovery learning is a teaching approach that is based on inductive thinking. It states that students work individually in order to learn the basic principles taught in a lesson. It involves many steps, such as asking questions, exploring, and gathering data, concluding and making generalizations based upon these conclusions. Learning is solely student directed and they learn through their own experiences and thought processes. It equates the process of learning with the answer itself. Students must understand how knowledge is acquired, especially how they do it, in order to better understand information and skills. Students will rely on the teacher for guidance in case they get stuck, but it is through their own discoveries that learning takes place.

Advantages and disadvantages of discovery learning

One of the advantages of discovery learning is that there is an active involvement of the learner in the learning process. Through their own experimentation and thinking will they come to the conclusion of the activity, often learning as much through the process as the end result. It also encourages curiosity and enables the students to develop lifelong problem solving skills. It can be highly motivating for some students as it allows them to discover their own ways to solve problems as it builds on their previous knowledge and experience. Disadvantages include that some students will find it difficult to learn without constant guidance and support. They may find it frustrating and give up easily unless a clear framework has been provided to help them find their course.

Whole group discussion

A whole group discussion consists of the teacher and the students, where the students are usually contributing comments that are directed by the teacher. Effective whole group discussion should involve planning on the part of the teacher and the students. The teacher might outline how the discussion should develop, using key terms and ideas, and the students might think of ideas and topics to contribute to the discussion in order for it to flow smoothly. It may be helpful to have a group discussion at the beginning of a class to get ideas flowing and to summarize what information has been previously studied. It can also be the springboard into small group work or independent work.

In a whole group discussion, it is important that the teacher sees his role as a facilitator in order to make sure that all students feel safe participating and that they all have the opportunity to do so. It is important to make sure that there are no students who are dominating the discussion and that all students have the chance to participate. If there are students who are wary of speaking in public, they could be given the chance to research what they want to say in advance so that they feel more prepared. Students should be encouraged to raise their hands, and the teacher should make sure that not one area of the room is receiving preference for contributing to make sure that all students have equal access. Alternating boy-girl-boy can be an effective way to make sure that one sex is not contributing more than the other.

Independent learning

Independent learning, or study, is the theory by which learners acquire knowledge solely through their own efforts and through this develop the ability for inquiry and critical thinking. Students must feel enabled by their teachers, meaning that they must have practice knowing how to persevere through problems on their own before asking for help from the teacher. They must be able to recognize their own faults as a learner and be held accountable for their own actions and inactions. Being exposed to effective ways to self-manage can be helpful for students who struggle working independently. Often the process of independent learning is as important as the goal of the task itself.

Advantages and disadvantages of independent learning

Students who can effectively learn independently will experience many positive side effects. Through their own processes, they will learn valuable life skills that transfer to almost any area in life. They are able to use the learning style that suits them best, and self-direction leads to higher order thinking. It mirrors learning in real life, for as adults, there will not always be someone there to guide one through life. However, there are also disadvantages to independent learning. Some students will feel discouraged by the lack of structure if they are unable to provide it for themselves. Also, some students feel that teachers should be directing them, not leaving them up to their own devices. There may be a low number of students in a classroom who are actually naturally self-directing, and the rest expect to be told what to do.

Teacher's role in independent learning

Even though independent learning seems to imply that the teacher is absent from the learning process, the teacher actually plays a very important role in the process. The learning environment created by the teacher must be supportive and encouraging in order for the students to feel safe experimenting and using their imagination when learning. It is also important that there is a positive relationship between the teacher and the students in order for the teacher to help students acquire a base of knowledge from which they can then direct their own learning. The teacher must ensure that students are ready to work independently, and scaffold the learning of those who need more assistance. Finally, teaching and modeling of skills must be done in order for the students to see what they can accomplish. Some students will need to see possible outcomes before they will accomplish a task on their own.

Interdisciplinary instruction

Interdisciplinary instruction is when students are taught, and able to understand, the underlying relationships that connect what is taught in each subject. When the objectives of the lessons are clearly connected, then the higher the level of student learning is likely to occur. For example, in an art class, students might be looking at the art of a specific time period that is also being discussed in history class. By having the same time period studied in two different classes, there is a higher chance that students will see the connections and retain the information. Interdisciplinary instruction also allows students to learn the information multiple times, and the very repetition of the material will improve the learning of the students alone.

Developing interdisciplinary lessons

There are several ways to develop interdisciplinary lessons. The first is to ensure that the objectives of the lesson are clear at the beginning of the lesson. This will clarify the goal of the lesson and make sure that the teacher is clear as to what the students should be learning. Second is selecting the content that will serve as the basis for the lesson, whether it be literature or a scientific principle. Third, identify other disciplines that related to the original idea, either with colleagues or on your own. Often natural links will occur, but asking other teachers will give a fresh perspective on the idea. Lastly, determine how the two or more disciplines correspond with the objectives in mind. It is important that a goal is always in sight, as with so much information it can be easy for that to become unclear.

Three ways in which interdisciplinary instruction can take place are: thematic units, curricular connections and thinking skills development. With thematic units, the teachers organize their lessons around a specific theme, such as teamwork, respect, or fear. Teachers of objective subjects, such as math, may find it difficult to do this, but a solution can always be found. Curricular connections could work when teachers of different classes want to focus on many aspects of one idea. They may plan to do this at the same time, or one after the other in order to link the ideas. Using thinking skills development can occur when teachers want students to use the same strategies in a variety of subjects. As long as students receive adequate instruction, it can be a valuable way to instill certain strategies.

Concept mapping

Concept mapping is used by teachers when they want to represent knowledge, ideas or facts in graphs or visual organizers. They can be divided up into a variety of categories. Concepts and links can be labeled, depending on how specific the information is. Ideas work off of each other and these maps can show the relationships between a variety of concepts that might not have been immediately clear. It can be done to brainstorm before a task is started, convey complex ideas, design a complex structure, assess understanding, measure where knowledge has not taken place, or aid learning by mixing both old and new knowledge. Meaningful learning is defined as the combining of old concepts and new concepts into existing cognitive patterns, something that can occur readily in concept mapping.

Inquiry method

Inquiry method implies that involvement in learning leads to understanding. It involves possessing and developing skills that allow you to find solutions to problems and issues while you are building on the knowledge you already possess. It is more than just asking questions and having a teacher respond. It involves several factors, such as a context existing where questions can be asked, a structure to the questions, and different levels of questions. It allows multiple intelligences to be learned because each learner can formulate their questions based on their own experiences in solving the problem. Taking data and putting into useful knowledge is a complex process, and involving students in this process will only make them more adept learners.

Advantages of inquiry methods

Advantages of inquiry method learning include that students are able to see how activities within a certain subject relate to other subjects; for example, persevering through a grammar problem can encourage them to try the same approach when solving a math problem. Students who participate in making observations as well as collecting, analyzing, and synthesizing information are developing useful problem-solving skills. They are also using higher order level thinking skills as they take information learned in a variety of subjects and come to their own conclusions. By developing minds that are used to inquiry methods, students will develop critical and creative thinking skills that will benefit them in real life experiences and enable them to think for themselves.

Critical perspectives of inquiry method teaching

Inquiry learning has been deemed as impractical by some because it requires so much time to take place. Since each learner can move at his own pace and needs input from the teacher, it can be difficult to regulate. Some think it is more effective for students to be given the information that they will need to know in order to survive once they leave school. Students must pass tests in order to prove their knowledge, and it is often not the type of learning acquired through inquiry that is on these tests. Emphasis in education should be on a core knowledge that is similar to all students of that age. These can be found in sequenced curriculums that tend to focus on facts and other quantitative knowledge that is able to be tested and assessed more readily.

Small group work

Small group work is defined as a small group of students who work together in order to complete a task or a series of tasks. When students work in small groups effectively, they tend to understand the subject matter more expansively. It helps students practice social skills, problem solving and communication skills in order to complete the task. They can be beneficial for shyer students who feel more comfortable speaking in front of small groups rather than in front of the entire class. Group work enables students to work at both the lower level and higher level orders of thinking as they often have to summarize, apply and synthesize their knowledge together in order to be successful. Students are also able to move at their own pace, and receive directions from peers in order to improve their learning.

Ways that small groups can be ineffective

The two main ways that affect the effectiveness of small groups is that they don't fully listen to one another and that the group members label each other. When group members don't listen to one another, they might tend to just believe that one person has all the right answers instead of thinking that everyone's viewpoint and ideas are valid. When people are labeled., it can make other members feel that their opinion is not important, but to instead rely on a few to do the work for the entire work if they are not entrusted with a task to complete. They might label the "brainy" student and have him do all the thinking, and not let the "slacker" complete any of the work in fear that he will mess up. By mixing up the roles of the group, it gives each member a chance to show their strengths and weaknesses, rather than just being prematurely and incorrectly labeled.

Successful small groups

It is important to allow time to teach students how to work in small groups effectively, just like any other topic that is studied in the classroom. The first step is to assign students to appropriate groups of about four to five members. These can either be randomly assigned, or planned

in advance to separate certain students from each other, and to mix up the social groups in the class. Making sure that the task requires group interaction is also important, otherwise one person may complete the task for the entire group if it was too easy. They should also know the purpose of the task so that they know what they should gain from working together. Having a time limit on the group also places restrictions and puts some pressure on them to complete the task.

During the time in which groups are working together, it is important that the teacher is visible throughout the classroom so that groups will stay on task, and that the progress on the groups can be checked without being too intrusive. By making sure that the content is clear and that they have no further questions, the students will be able to stay on task. If possible, sitting in on the group discussions will allow the teacher to see how the students are working together. The teacher can observe the group dynamic and see if they need any clarification or if they need any help. By reminding the students how much time they have left, it will redirect them to the task and ensure that it is completed properly and completely.

How group work should close

Once the task has been completed, it is useful to come back together as a large group and have the small groups present their findings. If other groups have issues with or questions about their work, the act of defending their work will also reinforce what they learned from the task. Using the board to summarize each groups finding will reinforce the ideas to the rest of the class. Sometimes having the students complete a self-reflection can be useful because it can help the teacher in planning the next small group activity. It can be comprised of a paragraph describing each individual's contribution, or a response to a variety of questions.

Project approach

The project approach is a set of teaching strategies that help teachers guide students through real world topics in an in-depth way. It is not unstructured and the task is usually well-planned. When the project approach is used in a classroom, it can be a highly motivating way to teach. Students will feel actively involved in their own learning and produce work that is of a high quality and of which they are proud. As it is often related to real-life experience, they will be able to apply their knowledge to a variety of situations, making each project completed helpful with skills that students will need once they have completed school.

Creating a project

The first step is to present information to the students that will serve as the diving board for the task. This could be a story or video that introduces a new idea to the students. Then they might think of ideas they have about the topic, and write questions they would like to be able to answer in the course of the project. Next comes the field work. This could be research at a library, doing an interview, or going on a field trip. It needs to investigate one aspect of the topic more closely and allows the students to stimulate their thought process about the topic. Finally, the students need to come up with some way to convey the new knowledge they have acquired. They may be able to choose from a list of ways, or come up with their own method.

Using the Internet

Most students will probably have some experience using the Internet before they enter their classroom. Using the Internet alongside of an assignment can give students the chance to hone their searching skills, as well as their overall computer skills. However, there should be clear guidelines given to the students before the Internet is used, to prevent misuse. If the students are using the Internet for research, for instance, it can be helpful to compile a list of relevant websites for them to then narrow down. Making sure that there will be a meaningful result will ensure that the students see the benefits of using the Internet correctly. By giving the students control and having them work in groups, it can make the best of all students' skills and help students who are not as proficient on the computer learn from their peers.

Local experts

Often when completing a project or assignment, students struggle seeing how it will benefit them in real life, failing to see the relevance between education and working. By including local experts when teaching a concept or unit, it can make the link between how learning in school affects the job attained afterwards. For example, while teaching a unit on law, by having a lawyer come into the classroom, not only will he be able to give real life examples, but he will also be able to interact with the students, answering questions, and exposing them to a new career. Local experts can also provide extensive background information on a topic that the teacher is unable to provide, thus enriching the students' experience.

Field trips

Field trips, an excursion whereby students physically go and participate in an activity related to their topic of study, have been in use for a long time as a part of educational programming. However, sometimes funding limitations or time restrictions cause field trips to be taken rarely, if at all. Well-planned field trips have an important part of an education, and when used properly, can provide valuable learning experiences for the students. Field trips provide students with first-hand experience regarding the topic of study. It provides experiences that cannot be duplicated in the classroom, and provides more information than teachers can oftentimes provide. They provide the students with unique opportunities to learn that which otherwise would not be available to them. The field trip should be designed so that the students can see clearly the link between the concepts about which they are learning.

The most important consideration is the educational value that the students will be able to gain. There should be clear learning objectives for the trip, and the trip should be developmentally appropriate for the students. When planning the sites, a place should be considered that will provide a unique learning environment for the students. Choosing a place that most students have already been to will take away the novelty of a place, and therefore researching this aspect is important. The interests of the children should also be taken into consideration. It makes no sense to pick a place, such as a pre-1900 art museum when the children in your class are mostly interested in modern art. It is best to pick places relevant to the students' interests.

Virtual field trips

Sometimes it is not possible, with limits in funds and time, to take students on a real field trip. In these cases, all that is required is access to computers and the Internet in order to take advantage of the numerous virtual field trips that are available on the Internet. Virtual field

trips are designed to be educational and entertaining and many of these sites can be included in small group work, independently, or as homework or extra credit assignments. Students can explore the sites at their own pace, often with a series of activities to complete, either right on the website, or as given by their teacher. Virtual field trips can be to museums or farms, or to the solar system or even inside a digestive system. They usually use audio and video segments, thus appealing to multiple intelligences and allowing many viewpoints.

Service learning

Service learning is the method of teaching, learning and reflecting that when used as a teaching methodology, fits into the category of experiential education. It combines academic classroom instruction with meaningful community service and attempts to achieve specific academic goals and objectives by putting them into the context of community service. Students learn real-life values by participating in real world activities, learning about citizenship and other personal life skills that are intangible skills. Sometimes school credit is awarded for service learning, whether it be in the form of credits or extra credit for a specific class. It requires the students to be self-reflective as they think and process their experiences in service learning.

Goals of service learning

It aims to connect theory learned in the classroom with action and experience. Having this experience occur in meaningful situations, such as direct service that is necessary and serves others, helps the students to see the direct consequences of their actions. When students assist others, it can build their self-esteem as well as the self-esteem of those they are helping. It builds

- 45 -

citizenship skills as the students must help in areas that are important and necessary. It also fulfills the goal of students seeing how their academic subject comes into play in the real world. By acting as volunteers, it could teach students that volunteering is important and rewarding and introduces them to new careers that they might not have considered before the experience.

Why service learning should not be mandatory

When students are required to do something, they often approach it because they have to and see it as something they have to get done. But, when they are able to choose whether or not they participate in something, those who do generally do so because of intrinsic reasons and those are the students who have the most to gain. If students were forced to complete some sort of service learning in order to graduate high school, for example, the problems that may arise may take away any benefits of the project. If the school does not have the resources to provide the students with good programs, then the bureaucracy can become a huge burden, and the students will feel unfulfilled if the programs are not developed effectively. Students may see the service as mandatory and required, and thus not feel excited about their choice.

Curriculum

Curriculum in education is defined as a set of courses and their contents offered by a school which can be determined by an individual school, local school district, or state. In the U.S., the basic curriculum of a school is established by each state, and the individual school districts adjust it as they see fit. It is based largely on teachers' past experience in schools, textbook manufacturers, teaching standards, and information from peers.

As emphasis moves to results and test scores, curricula seem to focus on "teaching to the test" rather than to the overall educational experience of the students, and quantitative skills that cannot be easily measured. Teachers who are able to tailor their curricula to their students will feel more in control of their classrooms.

In order to develop an effective curriculum, it is important that the teachers are familiar with its intricacies so that they are able to clearly see how it will be presented in a classroom. Curriculum goals and objects should be outlined and shared with all the teachers in the same subject and perhaps even in the entire school. This will allow all teachers to learn from each other and know what skills are being developed across the school. It will also highlight certain aspects of a curriculum that failed to be developed or focused on. There should also be a variety of ways in which the skills can be taught so that teachers are able to adapt the work to the students in their classes. Ability will vary by class, so it is important that all students have the same access to the information in the curriculum.

Emergent curriculum

An emergent curriculum is different from the traditional sense of curriculum that the teacher plans before the students start school, based upon the goals of the school district or the state. An emergent curriculum builds upon the interests of the students and focuses on what they already know and what they would like to know in the future. It requires the teacher to take time getting to know the class, and it is often spontaneous and reacts to the immediate interests of a group. An emergent curriculum is often dynamic as well, changing depending on what shape the learning of the students is taking. The teacher is not seen as the expert, but as the facilitator of the students' learning experience.

Antibias curriculum

An antibias curriculum is an approach that challenges preconceived notions and is an activist approach of eliminating sociological maladies in education such as sexism, homophobia, ageism, racism, etc. By addressing issues of diversity and equity in the classroom, an antibias curriculum seeks to unlock students' potential by making them aware of all the issues in a society. Its goals are to develop students' self-identity, to help them interact with students from diverse backgrounds, foster critical thinking skills about bias, and teach students to stand up for themselves. It needs a safe classroom environment so that all these topics can be pursued, and discussions in order for students to learn from each other's experiences and backgrounds.

Anti-bias classroom

There are four main phases that can be explored to ensure that an anti-bias curriculum can be successful in the classroom. Teachers must create safe classrooms, and by doing this they must confront their own biases, learn about how students view diversity, evaluate the environment in the classroom for the messages it conveys about diversity, and identify parents who would be willing to help implement this change. The second and third phases involve the teachers' nonsystematic and systematic incorporating of activities into the classroom that teach anti-bias attitudes, whether these be role plays or activities. The last phase involves the students being a part of evaluating whether or not certain aspects of the classroom are anti-biased, such as textbooks and other learning materials, and should involve parents in order to discuss these issues

with their children, creating real life examples.

Curriculum maps

Curriculum maps are the accumulation of all the goals, objectives and topics of the curriculum in all areas of the school. They are mapped out in order to see where they intertwine and are useful when thinking of ways for the skills to be applied in a classroom. It is also useful when comparing how the curriculum of one area, for example art, can coincide with the curriculum of history. It facilitates teachers to see how the skills develop over the course of the curriculum and when and where to scaffold the knowledge in order to focus on the key skills. This can be an excellent resource for teachers who are interested in doing cross-curricular activities or for teachers who are switching grade levels or subjects.

Curriculum maps, while useful for providing the entire school with knowledge on what is being completed in all areas of the school, can also be used for a variety of other things. Curriculum maps can be a good start to an effective parent guidebook as it will inform parents what their children are completing in each class and will assist them in helping their children with the work by increasing the school-parent communication link. If the map is displayed in a bulletin board, it can help students see the links between areas of study and help them to see the big picture of education instead of individual classes. They also help teachers and administrators analyze how they are spending their instructional time and help to determine accountability.

Curriculum assessment

Having a curriculum clearly mapped out can be the easiest way to determine which assessments would be an accurate test of the skills learned. Some assessments could include tests and be more traditional, or could range from being performances or a portfolio of all the work completed. Assessments should ensure that students are participating in a variety of activities so that they are able to display their strengths in a variety of ways. The assessments that tend to be most effective are ones that students are able to choose themselves, usually from a prescribed list by a teacher. This will ensure that the assessments are accurately testing knowledge and are not just an easy way out.

Behavioral objective

A behavioral objective is a clear and unambiguous description of the expectations for the students that will set out which behaviors are acceptable and which behaviors are not. There are usually three parts of a behavioral objective: student behavior, conditions of performance, and performance criteria. Student behavior outlines the skill or knowledge that should be gained as well as the result that the students will be able to accomplish. The conditions of performance is under what circumstances or in what situation the students will be able to perform the behavior, such as in an oral presentation, or with note cards. Finally, performance criteria is how well the individual behavior is done, compared to a standard that is outlined to the students.

How behavioral objectives appear in the cognitive, affective and psychomotor domains

Affective Domain
The affective domain refers to the emotional and value system of students. These are learned by receiving, responding, valuing, organizing, and characterizing a value. It could be an objective for students to be able to

receive constructive criticism and to better their performance.

Cognitive Domain
These objectives will refer to intellectual learning and problem solving as the cognitive levels are knowledge, comprehension, application, analysis, synthesis and evaluation.

Psychomotor Domain
This refers to movement characteristics and capabilities and could be used as a way for students to use different ways in order to present their information. It involves the use of motor skills, whether small or gross, and can add a three dimensional aspect to the way students learn.

Learner objectives

Objectives make the course provide focused, consistent, and clear evaluation criteria. With clear objectives, students will know what to expect and what is expected of them. Students should be able to see what they will be able to do differently at the end of a unit or a specific task if the objectives are set out in advance.

There are three things that should be considered when creating learner objectives: First, the focus of the class should be outlined so that students know what they will learn during its course. If the course is consistent in sticking with these objectives, then the students will respond well to the structure and feel that they have control over what they are learning. Students should also understand the criteria by which they will be graded, and know how to improve their performance if they so desire.

Learner objectives should be specific and clear so that the student knows exactly what is expected. If the objectives are clear, then they should be able to be

- 48 -

assessed in some way that can be quantified, such as giving a time limit to work on a project, or a page or word limit. As with this, the students should have some say as to whether or not the task is acceptable, so if possible, there should be some choice within the task so that the students will find the task doable and realistic. Having a time frame is also a good way to make sure that the task is realistic, and especially with longer projects, giving goals, such as writing five pages of a thirty page paper each week, can help students to structure their time more wisely.

General learner outcomes

General learner outcomes are the goals that are set for all grade levels and in all academic disciplines. They aim to help the students live productive and enriching lives. There are seven general learner outcomes. To be a self-directed learner gives one the ability to be responsible for his own learning. A community contributor understands that it is vital that humans are able to work together. Being a complex thinker means that one has the ability to demonstrate critical thinking and problem solving skills. A quality producer has the ability to recognize when one's efforts are of quality and is able to reproduce that level of work in the future. Being an effective communicator is also important in order to work well with others, and lastly, being an effective and ethical user of technology is important as well because technology is used more and more often.

Guided practice

Guided practice can be used in situations where the teacher wants to monitor student progress. It is usually an activity that provides students the opportunity to grasp and develop concepts or skills that have just been taught to them. This is usually something that is done individually so that the teacher is able to assess how well the students have grasped the concepts before moving on to the next topic. However, it is not just simply worksheets, or questions; it is applying the knowledge to activity that encourages the students to use higher level of thinking in order to show that they have learned the skills and ideas presented to them. It can be used to check understanding and to monitor how well the students have mastered the topic. The teacher will also be able to help students who are struggling with a certain aspect before moving on, as the teacher is helping students individually.

What guided practice would look like in a classroom

The teacher would introduce a topic and after doing a few practice items, the guided practice would begin. It holds each student individually accountable by having them show that they are able to do and understand the work. The teacher will be continuously moving around the room in order to check that the students are on task and working through the task correctly, as well as giving assistance to students who need it. If students are not monitored correctly, there runs the chance of some students not grasping a task that will be built on at the next step, thus causing frustration and apathy. That is why it is important that the activity set requires individual effort that can be accurately monitored by the teacher as he is walking around the room, and does not consist of multiple choice or true/false questions.

Independent practice

Independent practice occurs when skills and strategies have been taught in the classroom as a part of a unit or activity. Practice follows once an activity has been set and the teacher has observed the students independently working in order

- 49 -

to judge whether or not the skill has been learned. Independent practice takes place when new skills are to be applied in familiar formats and judges whether or not students are able to apply new information. For example, if students are learning about division, the teacher may teach long division by starting out with smaller numbers, and then give the students problems that contain more numbers than taught to see if they are able to apply the information effectively.

Homework

Homework is generally the time that students spend outside of the classroom completing assigned activities such as practices, reviews or applied skills learned in the classroom. It enables students to work independently therefore improving independent study skills. Homework can provide more practice time for tasks that students find challenging and extend the knowledge of students who have already grasped the material. It can assist teachers in knowing how the students are progressing with the material, and help them to help students who are struggling. If students are held accountable for the work they do, it helps them to become more responsible and accountable for their work. It can also be a time to engage the parents in the work and encourage parents to take part in their students' education, as well as knowing that the school has high expectations for each student.

Homework should never be seen as a punishment, so giving students "no homework" as a reward should be avoided. Make sure that the homework assignments are varied by having some be short term and others being long term. Having homework assignments that take too long to be completed should be avoided so that students don't see homework as a constant frustration. If

links are made to class work and homework, then students will see homework as important to the class and do it more regularly. Instructions should be clear as well as the consequences for late or incomplete homework. It should be corrected in a timely manner so that students will be able to track their progress and should also include feedback so students will know how they can improve.

Completing homework

At the beginning of the year, it is helpful to have a handout for parents on the expectations in the classroom, as well as with homework. In this way they will know what is to be expected and can assist their children as needed. Also including some tips such as how to set up a good study environment and ways for the parent to help with the homework can be good things to include as well. When the first instances of incomplete or late homework occur, it is important to contact parents as soon as possible so that the parents will realize that homework is important to the class. Having a homework diary or someplace, like in the back of a notebook, where the students keep a list of homework can help parents know what is expected of their children and enable to help them accordingly.

Transitions

Transitions are periods of time in which the activity moves from one stage to another. It could be the time period between when a teacher assigns a task to when the students actually start the task, or the time period between when the students enter the room and when they are sitting at their desks. Successful transitions require many things, including careful planning, teaching, monitoring and feedback. How to deal with transitions needs to be taught to the students just as any other classroom routine. For example, having a list of things for students to do after they finish a task before the other students can stop problems with behavior if they always know that there is something for them to do. Most students will respond well to knowing the structures for transitions, especially since there are so many on a daily basis that they will encounter.

Transition skills

Setting teaching routines is an important way to teach transition skills because it lets the students know what is expected of them. By modeling both incorrect and correct examples of what to do, the students can see clearly what is expected. Also, making sure that the teacher reminds students what to do before the transition occurs will refresh their memory and give them a chance to succeed. It is important, however, not to do this all the time, as students will always expect to have a warning instead of just sensing the transition. When students to engage in appropriate behavior, having incentives and specific praise should be given. By recognizing appropriate behavior and ignoring or directing inappropriate behavior, students will know what to do. Finally, by having the teacher actively scanning the classroom, and moving around, students will feel the need to stay on task because they know they are being monitored.

Problem solving

Problem solving is an important skill that is used in all classes. The best way to initiate the cycle of problem solving is to ask questions that will spur students into a dialogue about the problem which will work out how they will begin to attempt the task. If they know what the problem is first, and define everything they know about the task, then they will be better suited to attempt to solve it. If they are able to visualize or imagine the solution, then their experimentation toward the means will have more purpose as they can see what they are working towards. It students are having trouble moving on, or are stuck, encourage them to take a break, by walking around if appropriate, or not looking at the material. Once a solution is found, have the students write down as much as they can in order to avoid other complications that could appear while planning the solution.

Learning Centers

When gathering ideas for a Learning Center, it is important that the topic is chosen carefully. It should be used to complement a topic already studied in the classroom. Then all the resources available should be gathered, including videos, books, with as much variety in the format of the texts as possible. Once all the resources are gathered, possible activities should be planned and developed, requiring that the tasks are completed independently and with the objective of the task clear. Enough time should be provided so that the students are able to complete the tasks within an acceptable amount of time. Next, create a self-grading check sheet so that the students are able to record their progress through the learning centers. As soon as everything has been put together it is time for the students to complete the tasks. The final step is to complete an evaluation, including a self-evaluation completed by the students.

Laptop computers

Students may use laptops in the classroom, take them on field trips or go home with them. If they are used appropriately, laptops can help develop project-based learning and multimedia activities as students work to collect data, brainstorm or produce projects. Among the advantages of having class laptops are that:

1) They are portable within the school and outside of class.
2) They may be taken on field trips and used for investigations.
3) They can provide immediate data processing and graphic feedback.
4) Feedback and analysis that is immediate prompts next-step decision-making in the field.
5) It allows files to be shared.
6) The computers generate reports and projects.
7) They can provide access to experts through e-mail or the Internet.

Important terms

Cultural Blindness
Differences in culture or language are ignored as though the differences did not exist.

Cultural Imposition
The belief that everyone should conform to the majority.

Discrimination
Differential treatment of an individual due to minority status, whether actual or perceived.

Ethnocentrism
The inability to accept another culture's world view.

Stereotyping
Generalizing how a person is to be treated, while ignoring the fact that individual differences occur.

The Professional Environment

Resources available for professional development and learning

- Professional literature - books and publications are examples of literature that can help a classroom teacher.
- Colleagues - a fellow member of a profession, staff, or academic faculty; an associate
- Professional Associations - an association of practitioners of a given profession, for example NEA, NSTA, etc.
- Professional development activities – sometimes put on by a local or state school board to teach educators the newest trends in education.

Code of Ethics

Ethical codes are specialized and specific rules of ethics. Such codes exist in most professions to guide interactions between specialists with advanced knowledge, e.g., doctors, lawyers and engineers, and the general public. They are often not part of any more general theory of ethics but accepted as pragmatic necessities. Ethical codes are distinct from moral codes that apply to the education and religion of a whole larger society. Not only are they more specialized, but they are more internally consistent, and typically can be applied without a great deal of interpretation by an ordinary practitioner of the specialty.

School as a resource to the larger community

Our mission is to work with communities to ensure learner success and stronger communities through family-school-community partnerships. Through schools, individuals value learning; learn how to learn; demonstrate effective communication, thinking and problem solving; enjoy a better quality of life; are fulfilled; experience the joy of learning; and contribute to and benefit from the intergenerational transmission of culture. in supporting the educational role and function of local education agencies (and organizations), families, and communities increase local capacity to improve and ensure learning opportunities for the children and citizens of the community.

Advocating for learners

Public support for education is fragile. Poverty jeopardizes the well-being and education of our young people and some communities are caught in a downward spiral of cynicism and mistrust. Teachers must necessarily be advocates for education. One might become involved in efforts to change policies, programs, and perceptions to benefit learners; such involvement is crucial for educators today, for when they do not create effective channels of communication with legislators, the media, and community members, their opinions will very likely go unfulfilled legislatively. These consequences can be devastating to children and to learning. The stakes are simply too high for educators not to engage in advocacy efforts. Just as teaching and learning require commitment, energy, and perseverance, so too does advocacy.

Parental education

As families shrank during the last half of the past century, parental education rose. Among adolescents ages 12-17 in 1940, about 70% had parents who had completed no more than 8 years of school, while only 15% had parents who were high school graduates, and 3% had parents who were college graduates. Expenditures for education have expanded enormously since then, and the educational attainment figures have been turned on their head. By 2000, only 6% of adolescents ages 12-17 have parents with no more than 8 years of school, while 82% have parents with high school diplomas, including the 21%-29% who have mothers or fathers with 4-year college degrees.

Parental educational attainment is perhaps the most central feature of family circumstances relevant to overall child well-being and development, regardless of race/ethnicity or immigrant origins. Parents who have completed fewer years of schooling may be less able to help their children with schoolwork because of their limited exposure to knowledge taught in the classroom. They also may be less able to foster their children's educational success in other ways because they lack familiarity with how to negotiate educational institutions successfully. Children whose parents have extremely limited education may, therefore, be more likely to benefit from, or to require, specialized educational program initiatives if their needs are to be met by educational institutions.

Parents with limited educational attainment may also be less familiar with how to access successfully social institutions, such as healthcare, with which children and their parents must interact in order to receive needed services. Equally important is that parent educational attainment influences their income levels. Parents with limited education tend to command lower wages in the labor market and are, therefore, constrained in the educational, health, and other resources that they can afford to purchase for their children. For all of these reasons, among children generally, negative educational and employment

outcomes have been found for children with low parental educational attainment.

Student diversity

Cultural identities are strongly embraced by adolescents but they also want to be recognized and treated as unique individuals. Teachers walk a fine line between respecting cultural differences and avoiding overly emphasizing them or disregarding them altogether. Responding to discriminatory comments immediately, using a wide variety of examples, quoting scholars from many cultures and identifying universal problems needing complex solutions can indirectly communicate appreciation of and respect for all cultures. Teachers must take care never to imply any kind of stereotype or make comments that might indicate a cultural bias. They must refrain from asking a student to respond as a member of a particular culture, class or country. Teachers should learn as much as they can about every racial, ethnic and cultural group represented in their classroom. It is also important that teachers respect students' commitments and obligations away from school, their family responsibilities and job pressures.

Cultural influences

Study after study has shown that a student's culture has a direct impact on learning. Since educational standards are based on white, middle class cultural identification, students who do not fall into that demographic face challenges every day. It's not that these students are incapable of learning; they simply judge that which is important and how they express that importance differently. Sometimes it is difficult for them to understand and relate to curriculum content, teaching methods and social skills required because their culture does things differently, emphasizes different choices and rewards different behavior.

Adolescents identify with their culture; they become what they know. If teachers ignore cultural differences, it causes communication issues, inhibits learning and increases the potential for behavior problems. As long as a child has no physical or mental health issues, he is capable of learning. He simply needs that the information presented and examples used to be relevant to his life experiences; otherwise, it does not seem to make sense to him.

Social environment

The social environment is the set of people and institutions with which one associates and communicates. It has both a direct and indirect influence on behavior by the individuals within the group. It is sometimes defined by specific characteristics such as race, gender, age, culture or behavioral patterns. When defined by behavioral patterns it can lead to unproven assumptions about entire groups of people. In America's diverse society, it is essential that teachers recognize that various social groups exist within a classroom and thus determine the best strategies not only to facilitate the learning of "book" facts, but also to encourage understanding and acceptance between the groups. The learning theory called social cognitivism believes that people learn by observing others, whether they are aware of the process or not. Creating opportunities for students to interact with diverse social groups in a neutral, non-threatening situation can bring about positive interpersonal growth that could have long-term societal impact outside of the educational environment.

Socialization

Socialization is the process of learning the written and unwritten rules, acceptable behavioral patterns, and accumulated knowledge of the community in order to function within its culture. It is a gradual process that starts when a person is born and, in one form or another, continues throughout his life. There are many "communities" within a culture: e.g., family, school, neighborhood, military and country. There are six forms of socialization:

- Reverse Socialization: deviation from acceptable behavior patterns.
- Developmental Socialization: the process of learning social skills.
- Primary Socialization: learning the attitudes, values and actions of a culture.
- Secondary Socialization: learning behavior required in a smaller group within the culture.
- Anticipatory Socialization: practicing behavior in preparation for joining a group.
- Resocialization: discarding old behavior and learning new behavior as part of a life transition; e.g., starting school, moving to a new neighborhood or joining the military.

The agents of socialization are the people, groups and institutions that influence the self-esteem, emotions, attitudes, behavior and acceptance of a person within his environment. The first agents are the immediate family (mother, father, siblings) and extended family (grandparents, aunts, uncles, cousins). They influence religious affiliation, political inclinations, educational choices, career aspirations and other life goals. The school's role is explaining societal values, reinforcing acceptable behavior patterns and teaching necessary skills such as reading, writing, reasoning and critical thinking. Peer groups (people who are about the same age) share certain characteristics (attend the same school, live in the same neighborhood) and influence values, attitudes and behavior. The media (radio, television, newspapers, magazines, the Internet) have an impact on attitude, values and one's understanding of the activities of society and international events. Other institutions that influence people include religion, the work place, the neighborhood, and city, state and federal governments.

Social ineptitude

Social ineptitude is defined as a lack of social skills; in most societies, this term is considered disrespectful. There are medical conditions that may cause a deficiency in social skills such as autism and Asperger syndrome. Someone who believes himself socially inept may have an avoidant personality disorder. A shy person or an overly bold person may observe societal conventions but still exhibit social incompetence; the behavior is simply manifested in different ways. The criteria for social ineptitude are different in different cultures, which makes it difficult to cite specific examples. People trying to integrate into a new environment may unknowingly commit a social faux pas thereby earning the damaging label unfairly. In a culturally diverse classroom, it is critical to create an atmosphere of acceptance so if a student does something inappropriate, the behavior can be quietly and gently corrected without causing humiliation or embarrassment.

Social skills

Social skills are the tools used to interact and communicate with others. They are learned during the socialization process and are both verbal and non-verbal. These skills are integral to becoming an active and accepted member of any environment. There are general skills needed to complete daily transactions such as being able to ask sensible questions and provide logical answers and knowing how to read and write and understand simple directions. If these skills are missing or poorly executed, it can cause various problems and misunderstandings, some of which could have long-lasting and/or life-changing consequences. In smaller groups, other skills may be needed such as the ability to engage in interesting conversation, present ideas to peers, teach new concepts or actively participate in discussions. Using body language and gestures appropriate to the situation and the message, having the ability to resolve conflicts and being diplomatic when necessary are examples of advanced social skills.

Meeting with parents

Studies have shown that the more parents are involved in their children's education, the better the students learn and the fewer behavior problems one must handle. Teachers are an integral part of the process. It is up to them to keep parents informed about the academic and social progress of the students. Report cards only provide letter or number grades and are not designed to explore and explain how well the student is learning and progressing in the intangible skills like critical thinking, reasoning ability, study habits, attitude, communication with adults and peers and other social and interactive development. Sending home periodic progress reports is an effective way to keep parents abreast of changes. Meeting with parents regularly to discuss their child's particular progress and being available to answer questions are excellent ways to work together as a team to ensure the student benefits the most from his educational experience.

Parent/student/teacher agreement

If a teacher should wish to use a formal parent/student/teacher agreement as a way to involve parents, provide students with a written set of expectations and explain their commitment to a successful educational experience, there are several activities that can be included:

- Parent Priorities:
  - Show respect for and support of the student, teacher and the discipline policy.
  - Monitor homework assignments and projects.
  - Attend teacher conferences.
  - Ask about the student's day.
- Student Priorities:
  - Show respect for parents, teachers, peers and school property.
  - Put forth his best effort both in class and at home.
  - Come to class prepared.
  - Talk to his parents about school.
- Teacher Priorities:
  - Show respect for the student, his family and his culture.
  - Help each student strive to reach his potential.
  - Provide fair progress evaluations to students and parents.
  - Enforce rules fairly and consistently.

Many schools use some sort of parent/student/teacher agreement to ensure everyone understands the rules and agrees to abide by them. It can be as simple as requiring parents, students and teachers to sign a copy of the student handbook or it can be a formal contract drafted with specific activities each pledges to perform. Whichever format is used, it should detail each party's responsibilities. This accomplishes several goals:

- Parents are recognized as an important part of the educational experience. They are also made aware of what is expected of them, their children, the teachers and the administration.
- Students are given written expectations, which prevent an "I didn't know" attitude. It encourages respect for himself, his parents, his teachers, his peers and the rules.
- Teachers make a written commitment to students and parents to provide an environment that encourages learning. They list specific, observable behavior which they pledge to perform.

Levels of parental involvement

Some parents are eager to participate in their child's education, some do so only when required, and others avoid involvement of any kind. All three approaches can be a challenge. Eager parents may bombard the teacher and administration with notes, phone calls, emails and requests for information and meetings. Setting reasonable, well-defined limits may be necessary. Parents who only show up when specifically requested (e.g., semi-annual parent/teacher conferences, meeting with the administration about a behavior problem), might only be going through the motions in order to keep their child enrolled in school. They may be incapable of or don't really care to address any underlying issues; they show up because they are required to do so. Parents who are never available and impossible to contact provide no help or insight and offer no support.

Parent/teacher conferences

Basics

Parent/teacher conferences can be stressful experiences for both parties. But with a positive attitude and much preparation, they can be pleasant, provide a forum for the exchange of information and improve the educational experience for the students. The first step is for the teacher to be rested. Fatigue can cause an inability to concentrate, unfortunate misunderstandings and inappropriate reactions. If a teacher thinks parents might be difficult to handle, it might be wise to ask an administrator to sit in. The teacher needs to have a plan prepared with discussion points and copies of the student's work available to review. He needs to keep in mind that the parents may have items to discuss as well, and therefore the plan needs to be flexible and allow time for questions. The discussion should focus on the positive and present negative information with a "we can fix it" approach.

In order to avoid wasting everyone's time during a parent/teacher conference, there are several things a teacher can do to set the scene for a productive meeting. Make initial contact early by sending a note or newsletter home briefly outlining plans and objectives for the year and providing contact information (e.g., phone number, email address, days and times available). This tells parents the teacher is willing to talk and/or meet when necessary. When a date for a conference is set, the teacher should be certain to invite both parents. It is the best way to gauge how involved they are, yet individual family circumstances need to be considered (one-parent families, parents' work commitments, et cetera). Schedule twenty to thirty minute conferences; if more time becomes necessary, schedule a follow-up meeting. Develop a flexible agenda and gather necessary paperwork. Verify parent and student names just before the meeting.

Encouraging parental involvement

Every teacher needs to develop ways in which to involve parents in the education of their children. Some communication methods may be more effective than others depending upon the age of the students, the educational level and time limitations of the parents, and the administrative support and resources available to the teacher. Some schools encourage a parent orientation program at the beginning of the year, in which the teacher informs parents what his expectations are concerning behavior and outlines classroom rules. He presents a broad picture of the material to be covered, projects that will be assigned and homework requirements. If a meeting isn't possible, the same information can be conveyed in a letter sent home just before school starts or during the first week. Besides regularly scheduled parent/teacher conferences, a periodic newsletter, perhaps when report cards are issued, can be sent to update parents.

Being prepared

Parent/teacher conferences are the best time for candid communication. For the encounter to be productive, both parties need to be prepared to discuss the student's strengths and weaknesses, share any concerns and decide upon the best way to help the student meet required goals and reach his potential. Some topics to consider in preparation for this important meeting:

- The skills and knowledge that should be learned and mastered.
- Required academic standards. Give parents a copy to which to refer during the year, and explain these standards.Projects planned and assignments required to complete academic requirements.The evaluation

method, what data is considered and when progress reports are issued.How parents can help. Suggest concrete activities which they can do at home in order to encourage learning and support the teacher's efforts.Programs available for both fast and slow learners.What programs are available to prepare students for life after high school.

Things to remember
Try to use a table rather than a desk and chairs so that the parents and the teacher meet as equals; this creates a more relaxed environment. Start with a positive statement about the student and then briefly review the objectives of the meeting. The teacher should not do all of the talking; it should be a conversation, not a monologue. Avoid educational jargon. Many parents will not understand it or will interpret it incorrectly. Focus on strengths, give specific examples, provide suggestions for improvement and refer to actions rather than character. For example: "Sam turned in his essay the day after it was due," instead of "Sam is irresponsible." Ask for parents' opinions and listen to their responses. Use body language that shows interest and concern and make eye contact. Do not judge the parents' attitude or behavior, and consider cultural differences. Briefly summarize the discussion and end with a positive comment or observation about the student.

Conclusion
If either the teacher or the parents feel that there is more to discuss or that a follow-up meeting is necessary for an update on progress made, a time can be scheduled before the parents leave. As soon as possible after the conversation while the details are fresh, the teacher should make notes of the general discussion and record any specific actions that he or the parents agreed to take as

well as the parents' attitude and willingness to offer support. Any private information and/or family issues which the parents shared should be kept in the strictest confidence. If a cooperative relationship is to be established, parents need to know that their family business will remain private. It is very important and even required in some states that teachers report any indication of or concerns about possible child abuse or endangerment to the authorities. All teachers and administrators need to be familiar with the pertinent statutes in their state.

Cooperating with colleagues

To be successful, a teacher must be constantly cooperating with and learning from colleagues. There are a number of ways to do this; one is to set up regular meetings with them. Many teachers are part of a team of teachers who instruct the same group of students, and these meetings will therefore already be in place. If this is not the case, however, teachers should try to set up frequent meetings with colleagues who either teach the same students or the same subject. These meetings should not be the equivalent of teacher's lounge gripe sessions, but instead should be forums in which new teaching methods can be discussed, teaching content can be coordinated, and basic plans of behavior management can be established.

Peer review programs for teachers

Another way in which a community of teachers can foster professional improvement is through peer review. In a peer review program, teachers observe one another and offer suggestions for improvement. This is especially helpful when it is done among teachers in the same grade level or subject. Another teacher who is fluent in French, for instance, would be a great resource for a non-French-speaking teacher helping new immigrants from West Africa. Of course, in order for this sort of program to work, there needs to be a spirit of collaboration and constructive criticism among the teachers. Unfortunately, school politics and competitiveness often poison the relationships between colleagues, and make it difficult to offer or accept well-meaning suggestions. The best peer review programs establish a specific protocol for criticism and encouragement.

Mentoring programs for teachers

Mentoring is another professional improvement program that can be extremely valuable to a teacher. In a mentoring program, experienced teachers develop relationships with beginning teachers. The schools that use these programs find that they are able to retain a larger proportion of their beginning teachers. When mentoring programs are not offered, new teachers should ask a veteran teacher to act as a mentor, as a mentor can provide guidance on any aspect of teaching, from classroom management to lesson plans. New teachers get the most out of the relationship if they consciously remain open to constructive criticism. A mentor should observe his or her mentee directly in the teacher's classroom, but the mentee should also keep a list of concerns and questions to bring to private meetings. Teachers who accept advice and are willing to see things from a different perspective will grow immeasurably from the mentoring experience.

Peer tutoring programs

Another way that teachers can join with their colleagues in order to improve the quality of instruction is through peer tutoring. In a basic peer tutoring program, more advanced students work with the younger students on class work.

For instance, the members of a second-grade class might be paired with the members of a fifth-grade class. The older children will still be using many of the concepts that they learned in second grade, thus it will be beneficial for them to explain and demonstrate these concepts. The younger children, meanwhile, will enjoy working with older children and may be more receptive to the material when it comes from a source other than the teacher.

Peer tutoring relationships are especially fruitful when they are between students from similar backgrounds. In a modern class, there may be students from several different linguistic backgrounds. Some students may be the sole representative of their native culture in their grade level. If there are other students in the school with the same origin, however, they may be profitably united through peer tutoring. Also, peer tutoring programs are a great chance for students to develop their social skills; the older children will practice being generous and considerate of someone younger, while the younger children will practice being attentive and receptive to counsel. Of course, only those older students who have a good grasp of the content and are well-behaved should be involved in a peer tutoring program.

Field trips with other classes

Another way that teachers can band together is by arranging field trips with other teachers, as it is often easier to handle the logistics of a large field trip in cooperation with another teacher. Also, many field trips will have applications to multiple subject areas. For instance, a trip to a local battlefield could have relevance for American history, English, and Social Studies students. A visit to the local natural science museum could be pertinent to content in math, science, and history. It is always a good idea to encourage students to make associations between content areas. Furthermore, a field trip encourages students to mix with other students, forming social connections that improve investment in the academic setting.

Coordinating subject matter

One of the most positive ways for teachers to work with their fellow teachers is by coordinating subject matter. This strategy is often used in teacher "teams" in elementary and middle school, but it can also be effective in high school. Let us consider a brief example of how teachers can coordinate subject matter with great results. Imagine that you are a sixth-grade teacher. Before the school year begins, you could propose that the sixth grade uses "cities" as a theme. Each teacher can then construct lessons in their instructional domain that connect with this theme. As the teacher, you could look at texts that focus on life in the city. The history teacher could teach students about the rise of the big urban centers during the Industrial Revolution. The math teacher could incorporate some study of the various statistics and charts that are used to describe and learn about cities. If your school is located in or near a large city, you might also take some field trips so students can observe first-hand the things that they have learned.

Coordinating instructional content

The net effect of coordinating content seems to be that students learn more. Educational research suggests that all knowledge is associative, and people therefore tend to remember those things that they can easily fit into their existing store of information. If a teacher and his colleagues can link diverse disciplines together by looking at the same subject from a number of different perspectives, they can help students develop a well-rounded and coherent way of intellectually exploring the world. This is especially true for students, who will be encountering a dizzying amount of new information at school. If this material is disconnected and seemingly random, students will be more likely to forget it. Thematic content in multiple subjects helps avoid this problem.

Communicating with colleagues

An instructor should meet with his colleagues at some point during the year so that he can get a general idea of the structure and content of his colleague's classes. During the year, the teacher should stay abreast of that which students are learning in their other classes, and should note associations between disciplines whenever they arise. A teacher should also know when his fellow teachers are assigning major projects or exams, so that he can avoid giving important assignments on the same day. Many schools assign a certain day of the week for tests in each subject; e.g., math tests on Monday, history tests on Tuesday, and so on. If the school does not do this, the teacher should make sure that major projects and examinations are scheduled such that students are not overwhelmed with a flurry of work.

Relationship with school administration

It is important for the teacher to have a strong relationship with the school administration. The principals and support staff of a school are supposed to be there to make life easier, but they can only do this with cooperation. In order to maintain a happy partnership with the school administration, teachers should remember one guideline of great importance: namely, teachers should always report any significant problems immediately; these problems can include disciplinary matters, personal problems, or conflict with school protocol. In large schools where there is little one-on-one contact between the administration and the faculty, it is common for teachers to let their grievances fester in silence. The result is that what could be a cooperative relationship becomes poisoned by resentment and frustration. Teachers who have complaints or concerns about the way the school is being run, or who need help, should immediately discuss the problem with the principal.

Meeting with the principal

A teacher should try to avoid only visiting the principal when there is something wrong. A principal, like any person, will develop certain assumptions about a teacher whom they only see in times of crisis. Also, many principals will resent those teachers who they feel are constantly passing their problems onto the administration. Teachers should be referring problems to the principal only as a last resort. It is appropriate to let the principal know about concerns without necessarily asking for help. A teacher should try to check in with the principal periodically when things are going well in class, so that he or she can get a more balanced appreciation of the class' progress. When a teacher maintains a good relationship with the principal throughout the year, he or she will be much more helpful on those occasions of crisis.

Scheduling an observation by the principal

One great way to cultivate a positive relationship with the principal is to invite him or her to sit in on a class. A teacher should invite the principal on a day when a particularly innovative and exciting lesson is planned. It is a good idea to let the students know ahead of time that the principal will be joining the class, so they need to be on their best behavior. During the observation, the teacher should invite the principal to participate whenever appropriate. Many principals were teachers at one time, and will welcome the opportunity to join in with the activities of the class. After the class, the teacher should ask the principal for his opinion. As in relationships with other teachers, teachers should try to remain open to criticism and accepting of advice. These kinds of observations can be very useful for beginning teachers, who may be unaware of some fundamental mistakes they are making.

Relationships with teacher aides and assistants

Some teachers are lucky enough to have full- or part-time aides and assistants. When this is the case, the teacher should make sure that the aide is being used appropriately. For the most part, an aide should not be busy doing paperwork during class time. It is certainly useful to have another person to help with grading, but this can be done during the planning period or lunch. While the children are in the classroom, the aide should be another set of eyes and ears. In other words, the aide should circulate around the room while students are working. He can answer any questions students may have about the lesson, and can make sure that students stay on-task. Aides are also useful when some members of the class have fallen behind the others. The aide can assemble those students and give them a brief refresher on the recent material as the teacher instructs the rest of the class.

Frequent updates to parents

After sending this first letter home, it is also helpful to send home periodic notes letting parents know how the class is proceeding. If one has a small number of students, one may even be able to make personal phone calls to each parent.

Another way to stay in contact with many parents is through email; if one finds that all (or even some) of the parents in ones class have internet access, one may send out a short weekly update. Whatever format one chooses, one should try to keep parents informed of upcoming evaluations, field trips, and special events. If possible, one should personalize each message with some specific information about the child; this will convey the impression that one is taking a direct interest in the educational progress of each member of the class. It is important to make an effort to communicate both good news as well as bad. For many parents, the only contact they ever have with the school is when their child has gotten into trouble. One should occasionally make a call or drop a note to praise a student for improved academic performance. Parents will respond very positively to teachers who take the time to praise their children.

Keeping parents alert to student performance

It is also important to let parents know how their children are faring in class by sending home their grades regularly. Many teachers require students to take home their major tests and have them signed by a parent. Increasingly, teachers are posting student grades on a class website so that parents and students alike can keep track. Whichever method one chooses, one should make sure that one does not wait until the end of the term to let a parent know that their student is in danger of failing. As soon as any student falls behind, it is imperative to alert his parents so that a strategy for improvement can be developed. Do not assume that students will keep their parents informed as to how they are doing in class. Many students will claim to be doing well even if they know that this will be disproved by their final grade.

As a teacher, it is ones responsibility to keep parents informed.

Parent-teacher conferences

Another important part of developing a positive rapport with parents is the parent-teacher conference. Most elementary schools schedule these near the beginning of the year, often at the end of the first grading period. In middle and high school, parent-teacher conferences are not always mandatory, though they are recommended. If one is a beginning teacher, one may approach ones first conferences with some anxiety. It is important to remember, however, that both the teacher and the parent both have the student's success as a goal. It is important to accurately communicate a student's standing within the class. It is also important for both parties to agree on a strategy for maintaining or improving the student's performance subsequent to the conference. Conferences are meant to be punishment for neither the instructor, the parent, nor the student.

Teacher-parent phone call

When a student is struggling, contacting his parents should not be a last resort. Rather, it should be done soon so that the student's course can be corrected. Many students act out at school because of problems they are having at home; learning about these motivating factors can not only help one understand the behavior, but can lead to possible solutions. In any case, when one calls a parent to communicate bad news, it is important to always maintain a focus on the steps that should be taken for improvement. Do not call a parent simply to gripe. At the end of the call, make plans to talk again in the near future, so that everyone can assess how the strategy for improvement is proceeding. Always treat the parent as part of a team whose aim is the success of the student.

Open house

Another traditional means of making contact with parents is the open house. Most schools hold an open house at the beginning of the year so that parents can meet the teachers and see the classrooms. Besides being an opportunity to give information about the class, the open house is a chance for the teacher to present himself in a favorable light. The neatness and organization of the room is very important, as is greeting the parents as they enter. One should try to avoid getting bogged down in discussion with any one parent; discussions of individual students should be handled in another setting. The open house is a chance for one to sell oneself and the class. One should demonstrate the structure of one's class as well as present an appeal for help from parents.

Inviting parents to class

Besides the open house, parents should be invited to school whenever their presence will have a positive impact on learning. For instance, if students are going to be putting on a group or individual presentation, parents should be invited to attend. This is especially important in elementary grades, where the presence of a parent can be extremely comforting and motivating to students. Other instances where parents could be invited to attend school are field days, class parties, and field trips. Too often, students create a rigid separation between their school and home lives. Language differences reinforce this separation. By inviting parents to class, a teacher breaks down the division between the academic and the family life, and encourages the student to incorporate what he is learning into all phases of his life.

Incorporating parents into instruction

A teacher should try to take advantage of parents' special skills or talents, especially as they relate to different content areas. For instance, if one is teaching a science-related unit and one of the students' parents is a botanist, you should invite him to speak to the class. If one is teaching a unit on Social Studies and discovers that one of the parents works for the federal government, it might be useful to invite him to speak. Whenever possible, one should be striving to make course content relevant to the daily lives of the students. There is no better way to do this than by incorporating their family members into the lesson.

Consequences of poverty

In general, poverty has been found to have negative developmental consequences for children. Children in impoverished families may be at risk of educational failure because they lack access to adequate nutrition, health care, dental care, or vision care, as well as lacking access to educational resources that parents with higher incomes can afford to purchase for their children. Children whose parents possess less education have parents who are less able to find full-time year-round work, and the work they find pays less well. As a consequence, policymakers and program administrators in areas with large numbers of children in groups with low parental education tend to have children as clients who not only have parents with limited education, but who work more sporadically, and who have limited income to provide for the needs of their children.

- 64 -

Respectful, reciprocal communication

One simple way to communicate more effectively is to treat the person whom you are addressing respectfully regardless of one's own emotional inclinations. Exhibiting disrespect is almost never helpful, as it immediately places the listener in an adversarial, and probably hostile frame of mind, and encourages them to disregard or dispute anything that is said. This does not mean that one has to agree with everyone and hide any opposition which one may hold to their attitudes, beliefs, values, or positions; it simply means that one should state ones differences in a way that does not belittle another's. For instance, instead of saying "that is a really stupid way of looking at the situation," it is usually more helpful to say "well, I see the situation somewhat differently." Then you can go on to explain how you see it, without ever saying directly that they are "stupid" or even wrong, but simply that it is possible to see things in different ways. Reciprocal communication involves each party receiving equal respect for their ideas and views.

Inappropriate treatment of students

According to the U.S. Children's Bureau, "More than half (approximately 53%) of all reports alleging maltreatment came from professionals, including educators, law enforcement and justice officials, medical and mental health professionals, social service professionals, and child care providers."

David Finkelhor, Director of the Crimes Against Children Research Center and Codirector of the Family Research Laboratory at the University of New Hampshire says, "The key problem is that educators are confused about what child protection does and whether it does any good." Finkelhor, who has been studying child victimization, child maltreatment,

and family violence since 1977, adds, "There is the other problem that schools may not support the reporting process."

Reporting abuse

Teachers are in a unique position to observe and report suspected allegations of child abuse and neglect, but they are in a precarious position for educators - especially neophytes struggling to comprehend various community systems and the vast arena of child abuse reporting laws.

Educators should be guided by their school's internal administrative policies for reporting abuse. Sometimes, however, these polices can be confusing. Some schools, for example, encourage educators to report suspected abuse internally before contacting CPS. Nevertheless, state and federal laws mandate educators to report suspected child maltreatment-allowing school administrators to determine if a teacher's suspicions should be reported is unlawful. Because educators are not trained investigators, it is especially important for them to report suspected maltreatment and not assume the responsibility of determining whether a child has been abused.

Neglect

Neglect is the most common type of reported and substantiated maltreatment. According to the National Child Abuse and Neglect Data System, of the estimated 826,000 victims of child abuse and neglect in 1999, 58.4% - more than 482,000 children - suffered from neglect; 21.3% were physically abused, and 11.3% were victims of sexual abuse.

Whereas physical abuse tends to be episodic, neglect is more often chronic and involves inattention to a child's basic needs, such as food, clothing, shelter, medical care, and supervision. When considering the possibility of neglect, educators should look for consistencies and ask themselves such questions as:

- Does the child steal or hoard food consistently?
- Does the child consistently demonstrate disorganized thinking or unattended needs?
- Would observing the family in the context of the community provide any answers?
- Is this culturally acceptable child rearing, a different lifestyle, or true neglect?

Sexual abuse

According to CAPTA, sexual abuse is the "employment, use, persuasion, inducement, enticement, or coercion of any child to engage in, or assist any other person to engage in, any sexually explicit conduct or simulation of such conduct for the purpose of producing a visual depiction of such conduct."

Sexual abuse includes any interactions between a child and adult caretaker in which the child is used for the sexual stimulation of the perpetrator or another person. Sexual abuse may also be committed by a person under the age of 18 when that person is either significantly older than the victim or when the perpetrator is in a position of power or control over the child

Reporting child abuse

Reporting child abuse involves a complex array of dynamics. Individual subjectivity, personal perceptions, education, training, and life experiences affect everyone involved in the reporting and investigation process. To maintain objectivity, getting as many facts as possible is essential. Before calling, the reporter should have all of the important

information, including the child's name, date of birth, address, telephone number, details of the suspected abuse and information about the suspected perpetrator. Are there bruises or marks? Is the child at risk if he returns home? Callers should be clear about what they are reporting. Vague statements of concern limit the screener's ability when determining whether to assign a case for investigation. Educators need enough information to answer basic questions that will be asked if they call CPS.

Behaviors that would be detrimental for an abuse case

When talking to children about suspected abuse, it's imperative not to ask leading questions or insert information. A case can easily become tainted if anyone involved asks leading questions or fills in statements for a child. The incident must be conveyed in the child's own words. Investigators, attorneys, social workers, psychologists, police detectives, and judges will scrutinize statements for information that could appear tainted if a case goes to court.

A recent study published by the American Psychological Association examined how misleading suggestions from parents influenced children's eyewitness reports. Psychologist and coauthor of the study, Debra Ann Poole, says even children as old as 7 or 8 will repeat misinformation. "Apparently," she says, "general instructions to report only what 'really happened' does not always prompt children to make the distinction between events they actually experienced versus events they only heard described by a significant adult."

Work of Special Education Teachers

Special education teachers work with children and youths who have a variety of disabilities. A small number of special education teachers work with students with mental retardation or autism, primarily teaching them life skills and basic literacy. However, the majority of special education teachers work with children with mild to moderate disabilities, using the general education curriculum, or modifying it, to meet the child's individual needs. Most special education teachers instruct students at the elementary, middle, and secondary school level, although some teachers work with infants and toddlers.

Qualifications to be classified as a special needs student

The various types of disabilities that qualify individuals for special education programs include specific learning disabilities, speech or language impairments, mental retardation, emotional disturbance, multiple disabilities, hearing impairments, orthopedic impairments, visual impairments, autism, combined deafness and blindness, traumatic brain injury, and other health impairments. Students are classified under one of the categories, and special education teachers are prepared to work with specific groups. Early identification of a child with special needs is an important part of a special education teacher's job. Early intervention is essential in educating children with disabilities.

Gifted Children

Former U. S. Commissioner of Education Sidney P. Marland, Jr., in his August 1971 report to Congress, stated, "Gifted and talented children are those identified by professionally qualified persons who by virtue of outstanding abilities are capable of high performance. These are children who require differentiated educational programs and/or services beyond those normally provided by the regular school program in order to realize their contribution to self and society". The same report continued: "Children capable of high performance include those with demonstrated achievement and/or potential ability in any of the following areas, singly or in combination:

- General intellectual ability
  Specific academic aptitude
  Creative or productive thinking
  Leadership ability
  Visual or performing arts
  Psychomotor ability

Characteristics of a gifted student

- Shows superior reasoning powers and marked ability to handle ideas; can generalize readily from specific facts and can see subtle relationships; has outstanding problem-solving ability.

- Shows persistent intellectual curiosity; asks searching questions; shows exceptional interest in the nature of man and the universe.
- Is markedly superior in quality and quantity of written or spoken vocabulary; is interested in the subtleties of words and their uses.
- Reads avidly and absorbs books well beyond his or her years.
- Learns quickly and easily and retains what is learned; recalls important details, concepts and principles; comprehends readily.
- Shows insight into arithmetical problems that require careful reasoning and grasps mathematical concepts readily.
- Shows creative ability or imaginative expression in such things as music, art, dance, drama; shows finesse in bodily control.
- Sustains concentration for lengthy periods and shows outstanding responsibility and independence in classroom work.

- Sets realistically high standards for self; is self-critical in evaluation. Shows initiative and originality in intellectual work; shows flexibility in thinking and considers problems from a number of viewpoints.
- Observes keenly and is responsive to new ideas.
- Shows social poise and a mature ability to communicate with adults.
- Gets excitement and pleasure from intellectual challenge.

Meeting the needs of gifted students in the regular education (inclusion) classroom

Research indicates that the needs of students who are gifted can be met in the inclusive classroom under certain prerequisite conditions; for example, (1) the students are appropriately grouped in clusters or other homogeneous arrangement; (2) teachers match their instructional strategies to the specific learning needs of the students; (3) the students receive an appropriately differentiated curriculum or have access to the full range of curriculum. Access to the full range of curriculum may be achieved in many ways; for example, through distance education programs, acceleration, or specially designed programs. It is not easy for teachers to provide a learning environment where each child is working at his or her level of challenge, particularly in an inclusive classroom. However, homogeneous or cluster grouping makes it easier for teachers to differentiate curriculum and use strategies such as curriculum compacting that have proven to be effective. Additional strategies for providing effective differentiated instruction are discussed in the literature included in this frequently asked question.

What a principal needs to know about inclusion

Inclusion is the meaningful participation of students with disabilities in general education classrooms. To practice inclusion successfully the school principal and staff must understand the history, terms, and legal requirements involved as well as have the necessary levels of support and commitment. The word inclusion is not a precise term, and it is often confused with similar concepts such as least restrictive environment (LRE) and mainstreaming. Educating children in the least restrictive environment has been mandated since the 1970s, when it was a major provision of the Education for All Handicapped Children Act.

The law states that to the maximum extent appropriate, children with disabilities are educated with children who are nondisabled; and that special classes, separate schooling, or other removal of children from the regular educational environment occurs only if the nature or severity of the disability is such that education in regular classes with the use of supplemental aids and services cannot be achieved satisfactorily.

Oberti test

Court cases have produced guidelines that can be helpful in determining the best placement for a student. One of these is Oberti v. Board of Education, which specified three considerations for determining placement: (1) the steps taken by the school to try to include the child in the general education classroom; (2) the comparison between the educational benefit the child would receive in a general education classroom, including social and communication benefits, and the benefits the child would receive in a segregated classroom, and (3) possible negative effects inclusion would have on the other children in the general education class.

Behavioral disorders

Students who have emotional and behavioral disturbances exhibit significant behavioral excesses or deficits. Many labels are used to denote deviant behavior; these labels include: emotionally handicapped or disturbed, behaviorally disordered, socially maladjusted, delinquent, mentally ill, psychotic, and schizophrenic. Each of these terms refers to patterns of behavior that depart significantly from the expectations of others. In recent years, "behavioral disorders" has gained favor over "emotional disturbance" as a more accurate label leading to more objective decision-making and fewer negative connotations.

Emotionally disturbed childred

Estimates of the number of school-age children and adolescents with emotional or behavioral disorders depend on the definitions and criteria that are used. At some point in their lives, most individuals exhibit behavior that others consider excessive or inappropriate for the circumstances. Thus, frequency, intensity, duration, and context must be considered in making judgments of disturbance. Unlike some other educational disabilities, emotional and behavioral disorders are not necessarily lifelong conditions. Although teachers typically consider 10–20 percent of their students as having emotional or behavioral problems, a conservative estimate of the number whose problems are both severe and chronic is 2-3 percent of the school-age population. Currently, less than one-half that number are formally identified and receive special education services.

Disordered behavior

There is considerable agreement about general patterns or types of disordered behavior. One researcher suggests two discrete patterns that he calls "externalizers" (aggressive, disruptive, acting out) and "internalizers" (withdrawn, anxious, depressed). He identifies the following four dimensions:

- Conduct disorders (aggression, disobedience, irritability); personality Disorders (withdrawal, anxiety, physical complaints); immaturity (passivity, poor coping, preference for younger playmates); and socialized delinquency (involvement in gang subcultures).

In addition to these, other researchers discuss pervasive developmental disorders (including autism and childhood schizophrenia) and learning disorders (including attention deficit disorders with hyperactivity). Not all behaviorally disordered students experience academic difficulties, but the two factors are often associated.

Adapting physical education to include students with disabilities

Adapted physical education is an individualized program of developmental activities, exercises, games, rhythms and sports designed to meet the unique physical education needs of individuals with disabilities. Adapted physical education may take place in classes that range from those in regular physical education (i.e., students who are mainstreamed) to those in self contained classrooms. Although an adapted physical education program is individualized, it can be implemented in a group setting. It should be geared to each student's needs, limitations, and abilities. Whenever appropriate, students receiving an adapted physical education program should be included in regular physical education settings. Adapted physical education is an active program of physical activity rather than a sedentary alternative program. It supports the attainment of the benefits of physical activity by meeting the needs of students who might otherwise be relegated to passive experiences associated with physical education. In establishing adapted physical education programs, educators work with parents, students, teachers, administrators, and professionals in various disciplines. Adapted physical education may employ developmental, community-based, or other orientations and may use a variety of teaching styles. It takes place in schools and other agencies responsible for educating individuals.

Dual exceptionalities

Gifted students with disabling conditions remain a major group of underserved and under-stimulated youth. The focus on accommodations for their disabilities may preclude the recognition and development of their cognitive abilities. It is not unexpected, then, to find a significant discrepancy between the measured academic potential of these students and their actual performance in the classroom. In order for these children to reach their potential, it is imperative that their intellectual strengths be recognized and nurtured, at the same time as their disability is accommodated appropriately.

Children with one parent

Children with only one parent in the home tend to be somewhat disadvantaged in their educational and economic success. Children in immigrant families are much less likely than children in native-born families to have only one

parent in the home, but there is substantial variation across groups. For example, no more than 10% of children live with one parent among children in immigrant families who have origins in India, Australia and New Zealand, Canada, China, and the Eastern and Southern former Soviet bloc, compared to more than 30% for those with origins in the English-speaking Caribbean, Haiti, and the Dominican Republic. Similarly, the proportion with one parent in the home is 17% to 25% for children in native-born families who are white or Asian, compared to about 50% or more for those who are Central American and mainland-origin Puerto Rican. The variation in number of parents in the household appears to be highly associated with level of parental education. For example, among children in immigrant families, only 10% live with one parent in the high education group, while 17% live with one parent in the medium and low education groups. Among children in native-born families, proportions are 18% for children with high education parents versus 49% for children with low education parents. The proportion with one parent rises from 20% at ages 0-2, to 24% at ages 3-8, and then to 25% at ages 9-13, and 26% at ages 14-17.

Having siblings

The presence of brothers and sisters in the home is a mixed blessing for most children. Siblings provide companionship, but they must share available resources. Insofar as parental time and financial resources are limited, parental resources must be spread more thinly in families with a larger number of siblings than in smaller families. Dependent siblings under age 18 are especially likely to compete for parental time and income. As a result, family size can have important consequences for the number of years of school that a child completes, and hence, for economic attainment during adulthood.

Among families of diverse native-born groups, the proportion with four or more siblings in the home ranges from 9% to 11% for Asians, Central Americans, and whites, to 18% for blacks and American Indians. In contrast, among children in immigrant families, the proportion in large families ranges more widely—from a low of 4% to 5% for children with origins in India and China, to a high of 35% for those with origins in the Pacific Islands (other than Australia and New Zealand).

As was the case with the number of parents, the number of siblings in the home also appears to be highly associated with level of parent education. Those children in families with high parental education are least likely to live with four or more siblings.

Having grandparents

Relatives, such as grandparents and older siblings, and non-relatives in the home can provide childcare or other important resources for children and families, but they may also act as a drain on family resources. Especially in families with few financial resources, doubling-up with other family or non-family members provides a means of sharing scarce resources, and benefiting from economies of scale in paying for housing, energy, food, and other consumable goods. At the same time, doubling-up can also lead to overcrowded housing conditions with negative consequences for children. Taking grandparents, other relatives, and non-relatives together, many children have someone other than a parent or dependent sibling in the home. However, children in newcomer families are nearly twice as likely as those in native-born families to have such a person in the home. Children in white, non-Hispanic native-born or immigrant-origin families

are least likely to live with such other persons.

About 9% of all children in the United States have at least one grandparent in the home, and whether or not a child lives with a grandparent is strongly correlated with racial/ethnic and immigrant status. For example, living with grandparents is much less common for white children (3%-8%) than for nonwhite children (12%-22%).

Overcrowded home

Overcrowded housing has deleterious effects on child health and well-being, including psychological health and behavioral adjustment, as well as the ability to find a place to do homework undisturbed. Nearly 1 in 5 children live in crowded housing conditions (that is, with more than one person per room). But nearly half of children in immigrant families live in overcrowded housing, compared to only 11% of children in native-born families. There is wide variation among groups, however. Among children in native-born families, the proportion in overcrowded housing ranges from 7% for whites to 40% for Native Hawaiian and other Pacific Islanders. Among children in immigrant families, the proportion in overcrowded housing among white groups is about the same as for native-born white groups, while the highest levels of overcrowding are experienced by children in immigrant families from Central America (59%) and Mexico (67%). Overcrowding is strongly correlated with parental education and poverty across racial/ethnic and immigrant generation groups, suggesting the need to double-up with relatives or non-relatives to share resources. This appears to be especially true among immigrant-origin groups. Moreover, while overcrowding improves slightly for older versus younger age groups, these reductions tend to be smaller among

- 71 -

children in immigrant families, despite their initially higher levels.

School in need of improvement

This is the term No Child Left Behind uses to refer to schools receiving Title I funds that have not met state reading and math goals (AYP) for at least two years. If a child's school is labeled a "school in need of improvement," it receives extra help to improve and the child has the option to transfer to another public school, including a public charter school. Also, your child may be eligible to receive free tutoring and extra help with schoolwork. Contact your child's school district to find out if your child qualifies.

Caring community

A caring community is the way in which the school interacts with the surrounding neighborhood and town. In such a community, all families are welcome and the immediate area is seen in the spirit of coopcration between the students and their families. The populations of students who attend a school will tend to be diverse, and therefore all families should feel included in the community of the school. Individual students will feel included if they are treated well by the staff and their fellow students and feel that the staff has concern for their well being, and that they are valued. In order for this to work, students must feel that their input and participation is a necessary function of the school and that there is communication between all facets of the school and the community. Family and staff members work together to solve problems and the rights of all students are strictly upheld.

Constructing a caring environment in the classroom from the beginning means that insults and derogatory terms are eliminated so that students feel safe in the environment. Students should treat the teacher with courtesy and respect, and that should be reciprocated. Having interactions between students on a regular basis will increase the level of community in the classroom because students will get to know each other and not use prejudice readily. When appropriate, if the students have the chance to provide their input into that which they study, they will feel motivated to learn and share their knowledge with others. Balancing between teacher-centered and student-centered activities will spread out the activities and make students feel accountable for their own learning. Setting an appropriate way to deal with behavior will also increase the sense of community, in that students feel that they are being dealt with appropriately. This works reciprocally, as well, in that pre-set consequences for actions which are enforced fairly and regularly create a stable environment.

Zero tolerance

"Zero Tolerance" initially was defined as consistently enforced suspension and expulsion policies in response to weapons, drugs and violent acts in the school setting. Over time, however, zero tolerance has come to refer to school or district-wide policies that mandate predetermined, typically harsh consequences or punishments (such as suspension and expulsion) for a wide degree of rule violation. Most frequently, zero tolerance policies address drug, weapons, violence, smoking and school disruption in efforts to protect all students' safety and maintain a school environment that is conducive to learning. Some teachers and administrators favor zero tolerance policies because they remove difficult students from school; administrators perceive zero tolerance policies as fast-acting interventions that send a clear, consistent message that certain behaviors are not acceptable in the school.

Education law

One function of government is education, which is administered through the public school system by the Federal Department of Education. The states, however, have primary responsibility for the maintenance and operation of public schools. The Federal Government does maintain a heavy interest, however, in education. The National Institute of Education was created to improve education in the United States.

Each state is required by its state constitution to provide a school system whereby children may receive an education, and state legislatures exercise power over schools in any manner consistent with the state's constitution. Many state legislatures delegate power over the school system to a state board of education.

Compulsory attendance laws

The state of Connecticut enacted a law in 1842 which stated that no child under fifteen could be employed in any business in the state without proof of attendance in school for at least three months out of twelve. The compulsory attendance act of 1852 enacted by the state of Massachusetts included mandatory attendance for children between the ages of eight and fourteen for at least three months out of each year, of these twelve weeks at least six had to be consecutive. The exception to this attendance at a public school included: the child's attendance at another school for the same amount of time, proof that the child had already learned the subjects, poverty, or the physical or mental ability of the child to attend. The penalty for not sending your child to school was a fine not greater than $20.00 and the violators were to be prosecuted by the city. The local school committee did not have the authority to enforce the law and although the law was ineffective, it did keep the importance of school before the public and helped to form public opinion in favor of education. In 1873 the compulsory attendance law was revised. The age limit was reduced to twelve but the annual attendance was increased to twenty weeks per year. Additionally, a semblance of enforcement was established by forming jurisdictions for prosecution and the hiring of truant officers to check absences.

Homeschooling laws

States that require no notice
No state requirement for parents to initiate any contact.

States with low regulation
The state requires parental notification only.

States with moderate regulation
The state requires parents to send notification, test scores, and/or professional evaluation of student progress.

There are states with high regulation
The state requires parents to send notification or achievement test scores and/or professional evaluation, plus other requirements (e.g. curriculum approval by the state, teacher qualification of parents, or home visits by state officials).

No Child Left Behind Act

Title 1 of the No Child Left Behind supports programs in schools and school districts to improve the learning of children from low-income families. The U.S. Department of Education provides Title I funds to states to give to school districts based on the number of children from low-income families in each district.

Individuals with Disabilities Education Act

The Individuals with Disabilities Education Act (IDEA) is the law that guarantees all children with disabilities access to a free and appropriate public education. It addresses the educational needs of children from birth through age 26 and accounts for 13 categories of educational special needs.

FAPE

FAPE (Free Appropriate Public Education) is requirement coined in order to comply with the federal mandate, Public Law 102-119, known as the Individuals with Disabilities Education Act. More specifically, part B of the act, which mandated that all disabled children receive a free appropriate public education and as such a school district must provide special education and related services at no cost to the child or his parents.

Individuals with Disabilities Education Act (IDEA)

IDEA amended the public law passed in 1975, which was known as the Education for All Handicapped Children Act, or PL 94-142. This law ensures that all students with disabilities receive an education that is appropriate to them. The definition that IDEA gives to children with disabilities can include speech or language impairments, autism, brain injury, hearing impairment, learning disabilities and mental retardation. Children from birth to school age also have access to certain state resources, if their state participates in supplying such services. This may include speech and language pathology or family counseling depending on their needs. A written IEP is outlined for each child once they reach school age, and the main stipulation that it makes is that each child should be educated in the least restrictive environment, which may mean a regular classroom setting for the child.

As IDEA has been amended, each time more care has been given to the role of families in special education. There are several levels of parental rights given for the level of special education that their children receive from birth through age 21. This could be consent, participation in the educational decisions about their children, policy making and notification. Parental involvement for infants and toddlers with disabilities is especially strong due to the availability of services for the entire family.

IDEA sets out goals for how to achieve an equal education for students with disabilities. One part of it is that students with disabilities are educated in the least restrictive environment, the goal of which is to be educated in a regular classroom. They should be able to participate in regular education programs to the greatest extent allowed. Segregating students with disabilities can be detrimental to their social development, and IDEA feels that educating them is beneficial to all students instead of hiding them away in other classrooms or buildings. Even though social benefits can be strong, they must be based against individual circumstances and the best environment in which a student can be educated can only be judged on a case-by-case basis.

SED

IDEA defines a serious emotional disturbance (SED) as "a condition exhibiting one or more of the following characteristics over a long period of time and to a marked degree, which adversely affects educational performance:

- An inability to learn which cannot be explained by intellectual, sensory, or health factors.
- An inability to build or maintain satisfactory interpersonal relationships with peers and teachers.
- Inappropriate types of behavior or feelings under normal circumstances.
- A general pervasive mood of unhappiness or depression.
- A tendency to develop physical symptoms or fears associated with personal or school problems." The federal definition includes children who are diagnosed as schizophrenic, but excludes socially maladjusted children "unless it is determined that they are seriously emotionally disturbed." Although autism was formerly included under the SED designation, in 1981 it was transferred to the category of "other health impaired."

Section 504 of the rehabilitation act

Section 504 of the Rehabilitation Act (regarding nondiscrimination under federal grants and programs) states:

- Sec. 504.(a) No otherwise qualified individual with a disability in the United States, as defined in section 7(20), shall, solely by reason of her or his disability, be excluded from the participation in, be denied the benefits of, or be subjected to discrimination under any program or activity receiving Federal financial assistance or under any program or activity conducted by any Executive agency or by the United States Postal Service. The head of each such agency shall promulgate

such regulations as may be necessary to carry out the amendments to this section made by the Rehabilitation, Comprehensive Services, and Developmental Disabilities Act of 1978.

Section 504 protects qualified individuals with disabilities. Under this law, individuals with disabilities are defined as persons with a physical or mental impairment which substantially limits one or more major life activities. People who have a history of, or who are regarded as having a physical or mental impairment that substantially limits one or more major life activities, are also covered. Major life activities include caring for one's self, walking, seeing, hearing, speaking, breathing, working, performing manual tasks, and learning. In addition to meeting the above definition, for purposes of receiving services, education or training, qualified individuals with disabilities are persons who meet normal and essential eligibility requirements. For purposes of employment, qualified individuals with disabilities are persons who, with reasonable accommodation, can perform the essential functions of the job for which they have applied or have been hired to perform. (Complaints alleging employment discrimination on the basis of disability against a single individual will be referred to the U. S. Equal Employment Opportunity Commission for processing.) Reasonable accommodation means an employer is required to take reasonable steps to accommodate your disability unless it would cause the employer undue hardship.

Section 504 of the Rehabilitation Services Act

1. People with disabilities have the same rights and must receive the same benefits as people without

disabilities when they are applying for jobs or when they are employees.

2. All medical services and instruction available to the public must be available to people with disabilities.
3. They are entitled to participation in any vocational assistance, day care or any other government program on an equal basis as those who do not have disabilities.
4. Selection to college, job-training or post-high school education programs must be based on academic records, not by disability. For example, someone with a learning disability can take a modified version of the ACT entrance exam.
5. An appropriate elementary and secondary education must be provided for all students with disabilities.

Purpose of Section 504

Section 504 was enacted to "level the playing field"; to eliminate impediments to full participation by persons with disabilities. In legal terms, the statute was intended to prevent intentional or unintentional discrimination against persons with disabilities, persons who are believed to have disabilities, or family members of persons with disabilities. Though enacted almost 25 years ago, until recently Section 504 has been largely ignored by schools. Given the statute's tempestuous history, this is little short of shocking. Two years after Section 504 was enacted, advocates held highly publicized demonstrations on the doorstep of the then-U.S. Department of Health, Education and Welfare simply to get the Department to adopt implementing regulations. But since then, the statute, regulations and their mandate have been considered by many as the

"black hole" of the education law universe.

Differences between Section 504 and IDEA

There are a number of differences between the two statutes, which have very different, but complementary, objectives. Perhaps the most important is, as has been stated, that Section 504 is intended to establish a "level playing field" (usually by eliminating barriers that exclude persons with disabilities) whereas IDEA is remedial (often requiring the provision of programs and services in addition to those available to persons without disabilities). Thus, Section 504 precludes hurdles to participation, whether physical (e.g., steps that prevent a person in a wheelchair from accessing a building) or programmatic (e.g., excluding a child with hepatitis from a classroom). By distinction, IDEA is similar to an "affirmative action" law: as some have asserted, school children with disabilities who fall within IDEA's coverage are sometimes granted "more" services or additional protections than children without disabilities. The "more" and "additional" denote another important difference between Section 504 and IDEA. While IDEA requires "more" of schools for children of disabilities, it also provides schools with additional, if insignificant, funding. Section 504 requires that schools not discriminate, and in some cases undertake actions that require additional expenditures, but provides no additional financial support. For this reason, schools often drag their feet in providing needed services to children under Section 504, and are less hesitant to openly discuss the limitations of funding.

Section 504 and the ADA

The Americans With Disabilities Act (ADA), enacted in 1990, has deep roots in

Section 504. In many ways, the ADA is Section 504 "writ large." The primary difference is that while Section 504 applies only to organizations that receive Federal funding, the ADA applies to a much broader universe. However, with respect to education, the ADA's objectives and language are very similar to Section 504, and for this reason both statutes are administered by the Office for Civil Rights and considered essentially identical.

State assessments in the No Child Left Behind Act

This refers to the tests developed by your state that your child will take every year in grades 3-8 and at least once in high school. Using these tests, the state will be able to compare schools to each other and know which ones need extra help to improve. Parents can contact your child's school or school district to find out more details about your state's tests.

Adequate Yearly Progress (AYP)

Adequate Yearly Progress is the term which the No Child Left Behind Act uses to explain that a child's school has met state reading and math goals. Your school district's report card will let you know whether or not your child's school has made AYP.

Americans with Disabilities Act (ADA)

The ADA was passed by Congress in 1990. This act outlines the rights of individuals with disabilities in society in all ways besides education. It states that they should receive nondiscriminatory treatment in jobs, access to businesses and other stores, as well as other services. Due to this law, all businesses must be wheelchair accessible, having a ramp that fits the standards of the law, and making sure that all doors are wide enough and that bathrooms can be maneuvered by someone in a wheelchair. If these rules

are not followed, businesses can be subject to large fines until these modifications have been complied with. The ADA also ensures fair treatment when applying for jobs to make sure that there is no unfair discrimination for any person with a disability who is applying to the job.

Title 20

Title 20 states that denial of equal access is prohibited. More precisely:

- Restriction of limited open forum on basis of religious, political, philosophical, or other speech content is prohibited. It shall be unlawful for any public secondary school which receives Federal financial assistance and which has a limited open forum to deny equal access or a fair opportunity to, or discriminate against, any students who wish to conduct a meeting within that limited open forum on the basis of the religious, political, philosophical, or other content of the speech at such meetings.

Soler and Peters (1993) as it relates to confidentiality

Confidentiality provisions help protect families from embarrassing disclosures, discrimination against themselves or their children, differential treatment, and threats to family and job security. Confidentiality provisions also may encourage students or families to take advantage of services designed to help them.

Many of the legal protections to confidentiality are constitutionally based in the fundamental right "to be let alone". Right-to-privacy protections also are reflected in federal and state statutes, statutory privileges, agency regulations, ethical standards and professional practice standards.

FERPA

A 1974 federal law, the Family Educational Rights and Privacy Act (FERPA), protects the privacy interests of students in elementary and secondary schools (and their parents) with regard to certain types of education records. FERPA requires that prior consent be obtained from the student (if 18 or older) or the student's parents before certain types of information can be released from school records. FERPA also gives parents and students access to records, along with the right to challenge the accuracy of those records and make necessary modifications. Changes to FERPA most recently were enacted as part of the Improving Schools Act of 1994, resulting in the issuance of final regulations of FERPA by the U.S. Department of Education. These amendments help promote information sharing by educators.

Child Abuse Prevention and Treatment Act (CAPTA)

The federal Child Abuse Prevention and Treatment Act (CAPTA) provides a foundation for states by identifying a minimum set of acts or behaviors that characterize maltreatment. CAPTA also defines what acts are considered physical abuse, neglect, and sexual abuse. Individual states determine and define what warrants further investigation. Civil laws, or statutes, describe the circumstances and conditions that obligate mandated reporters to report known or suspected cases of abuse, with each state providing definitions.

Physical abuse is an intentional injury to a child by the caretaker. It may include but is not limited to burning, beating, kicking, and punching. It is usually the easiest to

identify because it often leaves bruises, burns, broken bones, or unexplained injuries. By definition, physical abuse is not accidental, but neither is it necessarily the caretaker's intent to injure the child.

Lau vs. Nichols

English as a Second Language students (ESL) comprise one of the most hidden failure groups in American schools. Due to their difficulty in understanding, speaking and writing English, they fall further behind in school and increasing numbers drop out altogether. In 1974, a group of Chinese speaking children had a class action suit filed on their behalf in San Francisco. The San Francisco school system allegedly discriminated against the students by not helping with their language problems. The Lau case did not make bilingual education mandatory, but it paved the way for other states to start bilingual programs. The U.S. Office of Civil Rights outlined the Lau Remedies, or ways in which bilingual programs could be instigated, mainly that students should be taught in their native language until they could benefit from receiving instruction on the English language.

Supplemental Educational Services (SES)

Supplemental Educational Services is the term which the No Child Left Behind Act uses to refer to the tutoring and extra help with schoolwork in subjects such as reading and math that children from low-income families may be eligible to receive. This help is provided free of charge and generally takes place outside the regular school day, such as after school or during the summer.

Highly Qualified Teacher (HQT)

This is the term which the No Child Left Behind Act uses for a teacher who proves that he or she knows the subjects he or she is teaching, has a college degree, and is state-certified. No Child Left Behind requires that a child be taught by a Highly Qualified Teacher in core academic subjects.

Equal Education Opportunities Act of 1974

There is a strong concern for equality in education. Within states this leads to efforts to assure that each child receives an adequate education, no matter where he or she is situated. The Equal Education Opportunities Act of 1974 provides that no state shall deny equal educational opportunity to an individual on the basis of race, color, sex, or national origin.

National School Lunch Program

The National School Lunch Program (NSLP) is the oldest and largest of the child nutrition programs operated by the Food and Consumer Service (FCS) of the U.S. Department of Agriculture. Since 1946, the NSLP has made it possible for schools to serve nutritious lunches to students each school day. States receive federal reimbursement and other assistance in establishing, maintaining, and operating the program. To participate in the NSLP, schools and institutions must agree to:
- Operate food service for all students without regard to race, color, national origin, sex, age, or disability.
- Provide free and reduced price lunches to students unable to pay the full price based on income eligibility criteria. Such students must not be identified nor discriminated against in any manner.
- Serve lunches that meet the nutritional standards established by the Secretary of Agriculture.

- Operate the food service on a nonprofit basis

To qualify for federal reimbursement, schools must serve lunches which meet meal pattern requirements specified by the Secretary of Agriculture.

The lunch pattern is designed to provide, over a period of time, approximately one-third of a student's Recommended Dietary Allowance for key nutrients and calories. Meals are planned to include foods from the Food Guide Pyramid. While there are different specific requirements for each age group, it is not difficult to plan good tasting, healthy meals that offer the required balance of meats, breads, dairy products and fruits or vegetables - while reducing salt, fat and sugar.

Practice Test

Practice Questions

1. In the process of determining the rationale of an objective, the teacher should ask all of the following except:
  A. Does this objective have an important learning outcome?
  B. Will this objective fit my planned activity?
  C. Will my students be able to use this knowledge in the future?
  D. Are the prior knowledge and skill levels of my students sufficient to achieve this objective?

2. Which of the following is the strongest signal for getting students' attention before starting a lesson?
  A. Say "Good morning."
  B. Say "Let's get started."
  C. Ring a bell.
  D. Use a hand signal for silence.

3. Besides signaling for attention, a teacher should set-up and open a lesson by:
  A. Stating behavioral expectations during the lesson.
  B. Helping the students to focus by explaining the objective of the lesson.
  C. Discussing ways the students can connect to the lesson through their personal experiences.
  D. All of the above.

4. Which of the following is *not* part of the process of closing a lesson?
  A. Extended practice.
  B. Review of key points.
  C. Preview of future lessons.
  D. Demonstration of student work.

5. All of the following statements are true about the evaluation component of a lesson except:
  A. Evaluation may be group-wide instead of individual.
  B. Evaluation must occur in some form with every lesson.
  C. Evaluation may occur on an on-going basis.
  D. Evaluation may occur again; for example, during a unit test.

6. In regard to the process of writing a lesson plan, which of the following is true?
  A. The steps of writing the plan may vary with the teaching model.
  B. Experienced teachers won't need to write down as much as new teachers because some actions become automatic with time.
  C. The lesson's opening, body, and closing should be written in order.
  D. Only the parts of the lesson to be presented to the students need to be written down, not necessarily the pre-planning and editing tasks.

7. There are differences among planned activities that are necessary classroom routines, activities that are fun and provide a break, and activities that are directly related to the curriculum. Of the following, which is an activity for taking a break?
   A. Singing a song.
   B. Packing up to go home.
   C. Playing math games.
   D. Taking a field trip.

8. Activity planning and lesson planning are the same in which of the following:
   A. The plans include an opening that motivates students.
   B. The plans provide students a chance to apply previously-learned skills.
   C. The plans can be designed for a whole unit.
   D. The plans ask for skills from different subject areas.

9. For teachers to be comfortable with student diversity and to help students to be comfortable with diversity, teachers should:
   A. Review the stereotypes they have learned and find ways to bring reality to these views.
   B. Study the cultures they encounter among their students.
   C. Encourage students and parents to share about their cultures.
   D. All of the above.

10. Ms. Brown has a diverse set of family situations and cultures in her classroom. Which of the following actions would *not* be sensitive to these families?
   A. On the class information form, ask "What is the primary language in the family?"
   B. On the class information form, ask for information using the labels "Mother," "Father," and "Siblings."
   C. Write materials to be sent home in the language of the home.
   D. On the class information form, ask for information using the labels "Adults in the Home," and "Children in the Home."

11. A teacher wanting to show items from various cultures to the children in her classroom asks a child of Chinese heritage to bring a coolie hat to school. The family is insulted by the teacher's assumption that all Chinese are/were coolies. What is the best response for the teacher once she has realized her mistake?
   A. Apologize and let the issue drop.
   B. Rescind the request to other families for cultural items to avoid more problems.
   C. Ask the family to send whatever it feels appropriate.
   D. Have the child make a coolie hat in class since one was not available at home.

12. Of the following, which is often the resolution to parent/teacher cultural conflicts?
   A. The conflict is resolved through compromise; i.e., both teacher and parents making accommodations.
   B. The conflict is resolved when the teacher changes her actions to address the parents' concerns.
   C. The conflict is resolved through parent education about American cultural practices.
   D. The conflict is not resolved and parents/teacher continue their own practices.

13. When teaching children from non-English speaking families, it is correct to assume that:
  A. Children will give up their previous language/culture in order to adopt that of the American majority.
  B. Proficiency in one language can help in learning a second, so language skills will improve if children are encouraged to be bilingual.
  C. Nothing is lost when the child's language and culture are not reinforced at school because they will be maintained at home.
  D. Linguistically different children are educationally delayed.

14. For classroom teachers, awareness of issues in the family situations of their students is important. Which of the following is *not* true about children of divorce?
  A. Children are almost always more traumatized than their parents.
  B. Of children from divorced parents, 75-80% do not have serious problems.
  C. Children from non-divorced parents have no fewer problems than children from divorced parents.
  D. Pre-school children are usually the most afraid and symptomatic of trauma when divorce occurs in their families.

15. Which of the following is a correct way for classroom teachers to give understanding and support to a child whose family is in turmoil?
  A. Excuse a sad child from classroom chores, knowing that the child doesn't feel like doing much.
  B. Discreetly avoid any discussions with the child that might open up painful feelings.
  C. Provide classroom activities and materials, such as clay and paint, that might enable the child to work through feelings.
  D. Keep the child from being alone and having time to brood.

16. Which one of the following statements about objectives is *not* true?
  A. An objective describes a learning outcome.
  B. An objective describes where we want students to go.
  C. An objective describes how to get to the outcome.
  D. An objective describes the lesson focus and direction.

17. Which one of the following statements about objectives is *not* true?
  A. Objectives are a communications tool aimed specifically at the students, not other audiences.
  B. Objectives provide a way to evaluate student learning.
  C. Objectives help focus and motivate students.
  D. Objectives provide a way for teachers to measure their own effectiveness.

18. Which of the following is a good example of appropriate content for an objective?
  A. Compare and contrast science fiction and fantasy.
  B. Complete Unit 6 in the vocabulary book.
  C. Describe the similarities and differences of setting between the stories "Wilderness Adventure" and "PS 139."
  D. Solve the arithmetic problems on p. 114 in your textbook.

19. Which of the following is *not* a good example of the type of verb one should use to express the desired behavior component in an objective?
    A. Calculate
    B. Know
    C. Define
    D. Predict

20. Which of the following is *not* a good example of a learning condition given in an objective?
    A. On graph paper
    B. During partner practice
    C. After completing the unit on World War I
    D. Given a list of European countries

21. Which of the following is *not* a good example of a criterion in an objective?
    A. As assessed by the teacher
    B. With no errors
    C. For ten minutes each day
    D. To the nearest whole number

22. Which of the following would be a mistake when writing a criterion for an objective?
    A. Setting performance standards high enough to meet skills expectations.
    B. Setting realistic standards and time limits to avoid frustration.
    C. Gradually increasing expectations of accuracy as time goes by.
    D. Setting no limit to time or amount so that students are not pressured.

23. Which of the following statements is true?
    A. Write objectives that describe activities or assignments.
    B. Write objectives with creativity and complexity.
    C. Write objectives that represent important learning outcomes.
    D. Write objectives in correct form so that they will be appropriate for the students.

24. Objectives should be designed to teach something that is worth learning. Practicing skills is a good learning objective if the practice is embedded within application opportunities. Which of the following, however, may be a pointless practice?
    A. Reading to practice word attack skills.
    B. Solving problems to practice number facts and computations.
    C. Writing a composition to practice spelling and penmanship.
    D. Copying definitions of words to improve vocabulary.

25. Higher-level objectives include all of the following except:
    A. Making predictions
    B. Suggesting courses of action
    C. Memorizing important dates
    D. Providing solutions to problems

26. Which of the following is an advantage of Instructional Objectives?
  A. Since an objective must have a measurable outcome, it is easier to have low-level, and thereby easily-measured, objectives.
  B. Writing objectives forces the teacher to think about what students should be working on.
  C. Once a teacher has established a pattern for writing objectives, they all tend to be the same.
  D. Objectives tend to focus on parts of the whole picture rather than complete knowledge.

In order to reach each student, a teacher needs to recognize the types of learners in the classroom and plan strategies that will appeal to different learning styles. It is important, then for a teacher to know which strategies coincide with a particular learning style. The following questions identify a learning style and ask about appropriate strategies to match that style.

27. Strategies for establishing a verbal-linguistic learning environment include all except which one of the following?
  A. Classroom discussions
  B. Stories told by the teacher
  C. Task Cards
  D. Word walls

28. Strategies for establishing a logical-mathematical learning environment include all except which one of the following?
  A. Conducting interviews
  B. Venn diagrams
  C. Thinking of probabilities
  D. Discerning patterns

29. Strategies for establishing a tactile-kinesthetic learning environment include all except which one of the following?
  A. Large floor games
  B. Syllogisms
  C. Dance warm-ups
  D. Role playing

30. Which of the following describes a student who is a tactile-kinesthetic learner?
  A. Enjoys building models
  B. Perceives patterns and relationships
  C. Listens and responds to the spoken word
  D. Interested in writing

31. Which of the following describes a student who is a verbal-linguistic learner?
  A. Likes field trips and physical exercise
  B. Exhibits balance and dexterity
  C. Shows a knack for learning other languages.
  D. Adept at logical problem-solving

32. Which of the following describes a logical-mathematical learner?
    A. Sensitive to physical environments and systems
    B. Interested in a career as a builder
    C. Interested in a career as an engineer
    D. Reads, speaks, and writes effectively

33. All of the following describe a visual-spatial learner except:
    A. Uses clustering as a brainstorming tool
    B. Highlights with color
    C. Enjoys playing with sound
    D. Uses visual memory techniques

34. All of the following describe a musical learner except:
    A. Listens and responds with interest to a variety of sounds
    B. Wants to learn to sing or play an instrument
    C. Wants to be a sound engineer
    D. Responds well to materials of varying shapes

35. When designing a Pre-K to Grade 3 classroom, the teacher should assess the room to identify its most quiet area. This area should be reserved for:
    A. Art work
    B. Science activities
    C. A library
    D. A puppet stage

36. When arranging a classroom, which of the following are basic principles to follow?
    A. Separate noisy from quiet areas with shelves and furniture.
    B. Place materials so that they are at the children's eye level and reachable.
    C. Ensure that traffic patterns do not allow running.
    D. All of the above.

37. Having a print-rich environment includes all of the following except:
    A. Writing classroom labels in only one language to avoid confusion.
    B. Making sure print is at the children's eye level.
    C. Displaying the students' work around the classroom.
    D. Having the teacher prepare materials in front of the students to model writing.

38. If a classroom looks messy and disorganized, the effects might be all of the following except:
    A. Children displaying disruptive behavior.
    B. Children having difficulty choosing activities from amidst the chaos.
    C. Children worrying less about being neat and more about the task at hand.
    D. Children having difficulty doing clean-up chores.

39. Pervasive labeling has the effect of all of the following except:
    A. Helping children learn how to organize and store materials.
    B. Helping children to feel successful by limiting responsibility.
    C. Helping children to associate words with things.
    D. Enhancing the print-rich environment.

40. Part of the emotional environment of a classroom is the relationships between the teacher and the children. Children learn and develop well in a nurturing relationship that includes all the following except:
    A. Remains consistent in the teacher's interactions with and expectations of the children.
    B. Firmly ensures compliance with rules and routines.
    C. Empowers children with choices.
    D. Provides feedback in a positive manner.

41. The emotional balance of a classroom can be upset by conflict. Appropriate methods for a teacher to use in handling conflict do not include:
    A. Gathering information and re-capping the situation.
    B. Allowing children to come up with a solution themselves.
    C. Letting the issue drop once a solution has been agreed upon.
    D. Dealing with the conflict calmly and with a quiet voice.

42. Effective management of children with behavioral problems would include:
    A. Preparing explicit instructions.
    B. Following up instructions with focused, active practice.
    C. Giving immediate feedback.
    D. All of the above.

43. During a lesson, which of the following is the best method for classroom management?
    A. Making rewards contingent on everyone doing well.
    B. Promising a treat for good work to be given at the end of the week.
    C. Communicating behavioral expectations clearly before the lesson starts.
    D. Customizing the consequences for misbehavior to fit each student.

Beyond the standard rules for classroom management, specific situations, such as lessons that call for movement or an unusual activity, necessitate further behavior management.

44. Considerations for additional behavior management include all but which one of the following:
    A. Re-arranging seats to ensure compatibility and avoid conflict.
    B. The teacher rather than the students selecting partners.
    C. On-the-spot corrections since you can't plan ahead for what might happen.
    D. Stronger reinforcements to keep students on task.

45. Additional behavioral management needs to be included in lesson planning in which of the following situations?
    A. When there will be multiple transitions during the lesson.
    B. When the lesson requires the use of lots of equipment.
    C. When additional or unusual materials need to be distributed.
    D. All of the above.

46. Behavioral management should include specific techniques for students who have difficulty staying on task. Which one of the following would *not* be appropriate?
    A. Allowing such students to walk around to look at the materials that pertain to the lesson.
    B. Assigning specific tasks to be completed.
    C. Using response cards so that all students feel compelled to be aware and involved.
    D. Not allowing peer helpers because they might harm more than help by distracting the students who have trouble staying on task.

47. Room arrangement is part of classroom management. Which one of the following is *not* true about appropriate arrangements?
    A. Students don't necessarily need to see the teacher, but do need to see the blackboard, poster, or whatever demonstrates the lesson.
    B. Desks should be arranged such that the teacher can get close to every student.
    C. Desks or tables should be arranged to fit the activity; for example, small group discussion or independent work.
    D. Teachers should select who sits where and by whom.

Good classroom management is good behavior management. If a teacher does not know how to manage time well or establish routines, there will be too many opportunities for discipline to break down.

48. In order to make the best use of time and avoid lags in time that would allow student restlessness, a teacher should:
    A. Check out equipment to make sure it is working before the lesson.
    B. Rely on standard clean-up rules to take care of the close of the lesson.
    C. Clearly announce rules for sharing and returning supplies before the activity starts.
    D. Have supplies or handouts ready for distribution.

49. The establishment of routines should include:
    A. How to turn in assignments
    B. What to do when finished.
    C. How to set up for partner practice.
    D. All of the above.

50. Of the following sentences, which one is a negative communication?
    A. Close the door quietly.
    B. Use your own ideas.
    C. Stop fighting over the crayons.
    D. Be ready to explain why your answer is correct.

Students want and deserve to be praised, but the way that praise is communicated can be a delicate situation. The next two questions deal with effective teacher communication of praise.

51. Students prefer which one of the following types of praise?
    A. Public praise delivered so everyone can hear.
    B. Private, quietly delivered praise.
    C. Praise for good conduct.
    D. Praise for effort even when the work is poor.

52. Which of the following is an incorrect way to deliver praise?
    A. Make a big deal out of the praise so the student feels special.
    B. Specify the accomplishment rather than say "That's good."
    C. Back up verbal praise with a smile and warm tone.
    D. Call attention to new skills or note progress.

53. Students will be more interested in learning when they understand how the knowledge and skills learned in school can be applied in their own lives. The teacher can help students understand this connection by effectively communicating:
    A. Examples from former students of that school.
    B. Examples from personal experience.
    C. Examples from famous people.
    D. All of the above.

54. Teachers can positively communicate expectations in such a way as to make students eager to learn. Of the following statements, which one would be the least effective?
    A. "We're going to think like scientists in this class."
    B. "You might not like this practice, but it will help you to get a good grade."
    C. "I know you are all curious about how to make a puppet."
    D. "This project is one of my hobbies, so I wanted to share it with you."

55. When presenting information, effective teacher communication is best achieved when the teacher uses which of the following types of phrases?
    A. because, for example
    B. not many, not very
    C. somewhere, somehow
    D. generally, usually

56. Which of the following is an example of teachers failing to communicate effectively with their students or other teachers?
    A. The students know the lesson's objective.
    B. Assignments for 5th graders are less demanding than those for 3rd graders in the same school.
    C. All 5th grade science classes are working on photosynthesis at the same time.
    D. Students have been provided with a grading rubric for their compositions.

A teacher uses a mnemonic strategy of showing a series of graphics. After each graphic is described and its significance or relevance to the lesson explained, the students re-create the graphics on their own paper.

57. Which of the following is a benefit of this strategy?
    A. Assists visual and kinesthetic learners with acquisition and retention of knowledge.
    B. Assists students with linking a series of events.
    C. Assists students with grasping abstract concepts through concrete representations.
    D. All of the above.

58. Which of the following is *not* a good continuation of this lesson?
    A. Use these graphics as a review for a test.
    B. Make a game out of the graphics such as timing students to see how quickly they can put a set of jumbled graphics in order.
    C. Grade the students on how artfully they can draw the graphics.
    D. Have the students pair up to check each other's graphics for accuracy.

59. Which of the following is *not* a benefit of flexible grouping practices?
    A. Allows students to work at individual interest levels.
    B. Allows students to pick their own groups for better cooperation.
    C. Allows students to work according to readiness levels.
    D. Allows students to work on specific skills identified as deficient through assessments.

Preprinted response cards or wipe-off cards are used by the students to hold up answers to questions posed by the teacher to the whole class.

60. Which of the following is *not* likely to be a result of the use of response cards?
    A. The use of response cards is a novelty that will soon grow tiresome.
    B. The use of response cards reduces daydreaming and increases on-task behavior.
    C. The use of response cards dramatically increases the number of academic responses per student.
    D. The use of response cards allows teachers to better monitor student progress.

61. Which of the following is not a component of using response cards as a strategy?
    A. Actively engages students in the lesson assessment.
    B. Can be used before, during, and after the lesson.
    C. Allows students to collaborate on answers.
    D. Enables teachers to find out what parts of the lesson need re-teaching.

62. Which of the following is a good strategy that a teacher can use with a student who has trouble maintaining attention?
    A. Provide preferential seating.
    B. Place the student in a study carrel to reduce visual distractions.
    C. Provide the student with headphones to reduce sound distractions.
    D. All of the above.

63. For students who have difficulty finishing routine assignments, the teacher should do all of the following except:
      A. Teach self-discipline about staying on task.
      B. Avoid playing games with the materials because they might add too much time to the task.
      C. Remove segments of the task; for example, don't require the student to copy word problems before calculating the answer.
      D. Divide the task into segments and allow the student to work on the parts throughout the day.

64. Some children have difficulty with a change in routine. The primary strategy for dealing with this problem is:
      A. Maintaining the same schedule as much as possible.
      B. Giving advance warning of changes such as a visitor or school assembly.
      C. Allowing students who are likely to be upset to stay next to the teacher or a friend who can comfort them.
      D. Teaching relaxation techniques.

65. The best approach to using technology in the classroom is:
      A. Expect to teach technology with your subject.
      B. Rely on the school's technology center rather than your own classroom.
      C. Use only the technology with which you are comfortable.
      D. Increasing technology will improve instruction.

66. Which of the following statements is true?
      A. Students who write compositions using the computer often take more pride in their work than those who use pen and paper.
      B. Spell check allows student to focus on content and not mechanics.
      C. Computers allow for almost effortless reorganizing and thus less time and energy.
      D. All of the above.

67. Which of the following should *not* be a consideration about using computers in the classroom?
      A. Does the state test allow for writing on computers?
      B. Is the software easy to use and fun?
      C. Will I have sufficient technical back up if anything goes wrong?
      D. Will behavior management be more difficult while students are on computers?

68. Considering that not all web sites are credible, when doing project-based learning, students doing computer research should:
      A. Find several information sources with different perspectives.
      B. Look for identifiable sponsors or authors of the site.
      C. Check for the date of the latest update.
      D. All of the above.

In the following group of questions, choose the statement that is *not* true.

69. The following statements deal with the availability of computers in the classroom:
    A. Numerous federal and state grants have enabled high poverty and minority schools to catch up to high socio-economic schools in number of students per computer.
    B. Only one or two computers available in your classroom may limit use to demonstrations and word processing.
    C. More than two computers in a classroom adds the possibility of doing collaboratives, independent research, portfolios, and research papers.
    D. Only about 30% or fewer students will have computers at home unless the family income is $50,000 per year or more.

70. On average, today's students who grew up with television, computers, and video games:
    A. Enjoy group activities.
    B. Participate infrequently in extracurricular activities.
    C. Love new technologies.
    D. Identify with parents.

71. When deciding how much technology to use in a lesson plan, teachers have found that:
    A. Students spend so much time alone with technology that they are sometimes better off with a plain lecture or discussion.
    B. Students enjoy electronic presentations because the information is organized for them.
    C. Students find presentations with lots of video inserts to be confusing.
    D. Students may not think critically about the content if they copy notes from a PowerPoint presentation.

72. It would be incorrect to think that because today's students are active technology users, they
    A. do not watch much television.
    B. surf the Net frequently.
    C. participate in chat rooms.
    D. play lots of video games.

73. Which of the following would be the most appropriate feedback for a teacher to give to a student if the student identifies a verb as a noun?
    A. The teacher says, "Well, that could be a noun."
    B. The teacher says, "That's a good example of a verb."
    C. The teacher says, "No, I asked for a noun."
    D. The teacher says, "Wrong again!"

74. Feedback should consist of:
    A. Specifying what was done correctly.
    B. Making suggestions for improvement.
    C. Adding a positive comment to conclude remarks.
    D. All of the above.

75. After a demonstration by the teacher, a student repeats the demonstration in front of the class. From the following list of actions, what would *not* be the best way for the teacher to give feedback?

A. Wait to give feedback until the end if the demonstration is short.
B. Give feedback on each step as reassurance before continuing.
C. If a mistake is made, ask for the reason for the mistake.
D. Re-demonstrate the correct step if the student makes a mistake, then have the student try again.

76. Besides teacher feedback, which of the following is a legitimate way for a student to get feedback on work?

A. Using an answer key.
B. Asking an adult volunteer.
C. Reviewing work in student pairs.
D. All of the above.

77. Good tests that assess student learning effectively can be difficult to construct. Of the following statements, which is *not* necessarily a bad practice in test making?

A. The questions unevenly sample lesson content.
B. The test is long.
C. All questions have the same level of difficulty.
D. The test items use examples from topics that are not familiar to all students.

78. Of the following statements, which is an advantage of multiple-choice tests?

A. Multiple-choice tests rely on memorization rather than understanding.
B. Multiple-choice tests cover content that is easily assessed rather than being important.
C. Multiple-choice tests allow more assessment of content than essay tests.
D. Multiple-choice tests often have question stems that might give away the answer to those who guess well.

79. Which of the following statements is false about short answer and completion items on a test?

A. Short answer and completion items take more time to construct than multiple-choice items.
B. Short answer and completion items are particularly useful in math and science courses.
C. Short answer and completion items are particularly useful for spelling and language courses.
D. Short answer and completion items present some of the same scoring problems as essays.

80. Which of the following statements is an advantage of essay tests?

A. Essay tests allow students to organize their answers.
B. Essay test grading can be highly subjective.
C. Essay tests can cover only a small portion of the material.
D. Essay tests favor students with good writing skills.

81. Parent involvement is a term that means:
	A. Parent education.
	B. Parent volunteers in schools.
	C. Parent service on fundraising committees.
	D. All of the above.

Questions 82 and 83 refer to the following information:
- Low-level parent involvement means that parents take part in activities that do not challenge the expertise of a teacher or decision-making powers of the school; and
- High-level parent involvement means that parents are provided opportunities to make their presence known.

82. Of the following choices, which show the *highest* level of parent involvement?
	A. Baking cookies for a class event.
	B. Going on a field trip with a child's class.
	C. Participation in a school intervention program.
	D. Attending a parent/teacher conference.

83. Of the following choices, which shows the *lowest* level of parent involvement?
	A. Parent visits to the classroom.
	B. Parent production of a school newsletter.
	C. Parent on-site observations.
	D. Parent volunteer assistance in the classroom.

84. Of the following choices, which does NOT mandate parental involvement?
	A. School-based parental education programs
	B. Head Start
	C. Title I
	D. Individuals with Disabilities Act

85. Of the following types of pre-school programs, which has mandated parental involvement?
	A. Child-care franchises
	B. Family child-care homes
	C. Head Start
	D. Non-profit child-care programs

86. Of the following choices, which has the *least* effect on student success?
	A. Good interaction skills of the parent.
	B. Socio-economic status of the parent.
	C. Self-esteem of the parent.
	D. Parent involvement in the student's academic programs.

87. For families that are low on the socio-economic scale and in need of support systems for successful child rearing, the school or pre-school should *not*:
   A. Assume the role of the parent until an intervention program can improve the parent's skills.
   B. Become one of the agencies offering services to the family.
   C. Establish an equal working relationship with the parent.
   D. Act as a form of extended family that supports the authority of the parent.

88. Teachers who have difficulty interacting with parents would benefit from:
   A. Preparing comments before meeting with parents.
   B. Sharing their fears with other teachers to elicit advice.
   C. Setting a goal to talk with a certain number of parents per week.
   D. All of the above.

89. Which is the least effective way to improve your performance as a teacher?
   A. Teach yourself with school or district audio tapes and videos on topics of best teaching practices.
   B. Subscribe to an education journal.
   C. Frequent the teacher lounge to listen to other teachers' experiences.
   D. Attend professional development conferences, seminars, and workshops.

90. The most important investment a school board, administrators, and parents can make in a school system is to provide teachers with continuous opportunities to learn because it:
   A. Deepens and broadens knowledge of content.
   B. Provides knowledge about the teaching and learning process.
   C. Is intellectually engaging and addresses the complexity of teaching.
   D. All of the above.

91. For teachers to master new content and pedagogy and be able to integrate this knowledge and skill into their practice, teachers must be given all of the following except:
   A. Time
   B. Pay incentives
   C. Support
   D. Resources

92. Of the following choices, which is true? Professional development is not
   A. site-specific since some principles of teaching are universal.
   B. about content but about strategies.
   C. necessarily job-embedded because it is an opportunity to explore other educational roles.
   D. designed by experts only but by teachers as well.

93. Of the following, which is the greatest challenge associated with professional development?
   A. Finding time to schedule professional development and do follow-up.
   B. Developing seminars on the implementation of new educational standards.
   C. Addressing the changing forms of student assessment.
   D. Providing guidelines for working with diverse populations.

94. Of the following, which is the best way to conduct professional development?
   A. Assigning the teachers to team planning while administrators have their own meetings.
   B. Doing professional development during the summer.
   C. Hiring substitutes to cover for a day of development for a group of teachers.
   D. Involving parents in planning professional development so they see its value.

95. Which of the following is the least-recommended use of technology for professional development?
   A. Watching video conferences to get seminar-style education without travel.
   B. Accessing collegial networks to exchange ideas with like teachers.
   C. Relying on distance education rather than on-campus or in-district opportunities.
   D. Using electronic bulletin boards for teaching and resource tips.

96. Which of the following is true?
   A. Pre-service training is adequate preparation for the teachers to do their work.
   B. The school district is in the business of educating students, not teachers.
   C. Teachers should spend at least 20% of their work time in professional study and collaborative work.
   D. To avoid taking time away from students, teachers should pursue professional development on their own time.

97. Laws and ethics are important areas of concern for the classroom teacher, starting with an understanding of the differences between laws and ethics. Of the following statements, which one is false?
   A. Laws are concrete, written and enacted by people.
   B. Ethics are less tangible and observable and consist of ideas.
   C. Laws are always ethical.
   D. Most laws are the codification of what society considers moral or ethical obligations.

98. Betty is a veteran teacher who has been asked by the principal to mentor a new teacher and report her observations. Betty discovers that the newcomer is a poor teacher with few disciplinary or instructional skills. Which of the following should *not* be a consideration for Betty if she is ethical?
   A. The new teacher's need for a job.
   B. Her obligation to the principal to give an accurate report.
   C. Passing off the mentoring job to another teacher.
   D. The children's need for a competent teacher.

99. Which of the following is an everyday way that teachers can ethically influence students?
   A. By setting an example in the way they do their work and care about their students.
   B. By establishing a classroom climate of respect and cooperation.
   C. By incorporating discussions of ethics into the subject matter of the lesson.
   D. All of the above.

100. Considering the due process rights of a teacher, which of the following is an incorrect statement?

     A. The principal must schedule a dismissal hearing at a reasonable time and place.

     B. A school district must justify its reasons for not rehiring a teacher, even if the teacher is on probation.

     C. The teacher must be allowed to confront and question witnesses at the dismissal hearing.

     D. The teacher must be given timely and adequate notice giving details of the reasons for the proposed suspension or dismissal.

Answers and Explanations

1: Answer = B. Lesson objectives should have an important outcome, should be useful to the students in the future, and should be at a knowledge and skill level appropriate to the students; however, activities should be planned to fit the objective, not the other way around.

Every lesson plan should be concerned with an important learning outcome - trivial lessons are a waste of time and damage student interest – therefore, all lesson plans should include an important objective. The knowledge gained by a lesson should also be something students can use in the future; otherwise the lesson has no point. The lesson should also be comprehensible to the students – teaching above their skill levels leaves them unsuccessful and frustrated; teaching below their skills levels leaves them bored.

2: Answer = C. Ringing a bell is the strongest signal for getting attention from the students. Just saying something might not be heard or might be ignored because the teacher is often talking, and a hand signal might not be seen. However, a bell makes a sound different from the usual human voice and is usually louder, too, so it makes the strongest attention-getting signal.

Good teachers establish certain signals with their students as a form of shortcut communication. The most common is the signal for attention. Simply saying "Good morning" or "Let's get started" are good oral signals that the teacher wants all eyes on him/her so that a change of activity can begin. Hand signals such as just holding up a hand as a signal for quiet also work well.

3: Answer = D. Answers A, B, and C, all describe appropriate and necessary elements of setting up a new lesson so that students know what the lesson is intended to do, how it can be of benefit to them, and what behavior will help them to succeed.

When a teacher starts a new lesson, it is critical that the objective of the lesson is clearly communicated, that the students are helped to make a connection between the lesson and their personal experiences, and that behavioral expectations are set.

4: Answer = A. Extended practice should be part of the lesson when the teacher's evaluation shows that extended practice is needed to solidify the lesson or ensure that all students have learned the objective. The closing of the lesson is too late to try to back up and insert extended practice.

When closing a lesson, it is natural to review key points, perhaps as demonstrated by work done by the students during the lesson, and giving the students a preview of the next or other related lessons builds student anticipation and desire to learn.

5: Answer = A. The teacher needs to know how well each student is doing and must teach each child. The teacher is striving for a quality learning experience for every child rather than averages or high percentages measured by a group-wide evaluation.

It is true that evaluation must be part of every lesson, in some form or another, or else the teacher will not know if the objective was reached, and if some or all students need a re-teach. This evaluation can continue with retention checks in other lessons; that is, on an on-going basis, and may be repeated in overall unit tests.

6: Answer = B. The lesson plans for an experienced teacher do not have to be as detailed as they should be for a new teacher because some actions become second nature to a teacher after a while and go without saying.

The steps to writing a good lesson plan do not vary with the teaching model but are the backbone of every lesson. The lesson opening, body, and closing do not need to be written in order; in fact, it is often best to write the body of the lesson first so that the teacher has had a chance to thoroughly think through the lesson before deciding on an appropriate opening. Since the lesson plan has a set pattern, all parts must be written, including pre-planning steps and editing tasks, not just the parts that will be presented to the students.

7: Answer = A. Singing a song is the answer because this is a pleasant activity that the children enjoy and that helps them to relax. Singing a song is good for a break, especially a break that transitions into a new lesson or activity. Although some songs may also enhance a lesson, the students perceive singing a fun song as just that: fun.

Packing up to go home is a routine activity that is part of the classroom management structure. Playing math games is an activity that is directly related to the math curriculum and reinforces a lesson. Taking a field trip is also related to the curriculum and is supposed to be designed to illustrate or enhance a lesson.

8: Answer = C. A lesson is only one component of a unit, so the lesson plan cannot cover the whole unit. An activity plan, however, can be for an activity that incorporates several components of a unit or is a good summary activity for a unit.

Whether an activity or a lesson, the opening should be something that will motivate the students to take an interest and participate in the lesson. The plans for an activity or lesson can give students an opportunity to apply previously learned skills in that subject or to integrate skills from different subjects.

9: Answer = D. All the answers are linked by the teacher's need to know more about the students' cultures. Inadequate knowledge that might lead to a misunderstanding with a student or parent needs remediation, first through recognition of any gaps of knowledge and then by various means of getting to know the cultures.

Most people's knowledge about other cultures contains some stereotypes. For teachers who have a multi-cultural classroom, it would be beneficial for them to think through what they know about the cultures of the children in their classrooms to analyze whether any of that knowledge is based on stereotypes. They need to question themselves as to whether they have any first-hand knowledge about these cultures. If not, they need to devote a little time to studying about these cultures. One way to learn is to ask the children and their parents to share information about their cultures for the benefit of all.

10: Answer = B. A home that has stepparents or relatives other than the mother and father might feel ill at ease with a form that asks for only those identifications.

Any teacher is likely to have a class with students who come from single-parent homes, who have divorced parents, who have stepparents and step-siblings, or who live with a grandparent or other relatives. The teacher needs to be sensitive to these various family make-ups by making forms and addressing letters in a generic manner that would fit any situation. For better communication in a multi-cultural classroom, it is a good idea to have forms and letters in whatever languages the children's parents' use. Asking early in the year about languages spoken in the home allows the teacher to customize communication to fit the response.

11: Answer = C. The offended family will be given the opportunity to educate the teacher and the class about their culture. The activity should continue so that the other students aren't denied an opportunity to share because of the teacher's mistake. Most definitely, the teacher should not compound the error by persisting in asking for something that s/he has been told is offensive.

Teachers who make assumptions based on cultural stereotypes could offend students with inappropriate statements or requests. It is good practice to have the students share about their cultures in a "Show and Tell" activity, for example. However, should the teacher make a mistake about cultural practices, s/he should apologize to anyone offended and not let the matter drop but follow up with another option and continue the activity for everyone. The teacher should give careful thought to the mistake and correct any misconceptions.

12: Answer = D. Unfortunately, it is fairly common that no one tries to resolve the problem. Through fear of speaking up or ignorance of the problem, the situation continues and irritates all concerned.

There are a variety of ways to solve a conflict. One is through mutual compromise; another is for one side to change. In the case of a parent/teacher cultural conflict, there could be give-and-take on both sides, or the teacher could adjust to the cultural needs of the family, or, when the demands of the classroom cannot accommodate the cultural demands, the parents can be helped to come to an understanding of the requirements through education.

13: Answer = B. It has been shown that knowledge about the structure of one language makes it easier to pick up the structure of another. The other answer choices all play on prejudices or lack of knowledge about the best way to foster bilingualism.

Schools used to discourage the use of any language but English. Some people, even teachers, still hold strong views about English-only in schools; that immigrants are an uneducated, backward group; and that assimilation into the majority culture is the best practice. This question addresses those biases while testing the knowledge of the teacher about the value of multi-language education.

14: Answer = C. Children from non-divorced families do have fewer problems than children from families of divorce. The statistic showing that the majority of children of divorce do not have serious problems may lead one to think that they do not have any more problems than children of non-divorced families.

With a divorce rate of 50% in the Unites States, it is important for teachers to be cognizant of the consequences of divorce on their students. This question tests the teacher's knowledge versus assumptions about children of divorce. While it is true that children are more traumatized than the parents in a divorce, and that pre-school children are affected more than older children, nonetheless, the majority of children in a divorce situation do not have serious problems as a result. Still, they have more problems than children whose parents remain married.

15: Answer = C. Providing an outlet for the child to express feelings includes providing classroom activities and materials that would allow the child to draw or build something that is representative of that child's feelings.

Sensitivity to children who are in unsettled situations at home is very important for the classroom teacher. This question addresses appropriate reactions when the teacher knows a child is in turmoil at home. In such situations, it is wise for the teacher to maintain structure for the child; excusing the child from regular classroom chores would not be a good idea. It is wise to let a child talk out feelings, so avoiding discussing feelings with the child would be to deny the child a safe outlet. Troubled children also need time to be alone, so the teacher needs to know when not to push the child into activities.

16: Answer = C. The teacher is trying to communicate to the students what the learning outcome is, not how to get there. The lesson itself provides the "how."

An objective is defined as a clearly described learning outcome so that students know what they are expected to learn. It is an outline of where the teacher wants the students to go in their learning that day in class. Writing an objective on the board gives the lesson focus and direction that also helps in the selection of appropriate practice activities and evaluations.

17: Answer = A. The objective is like a public declaration for all to see – not only the students, but also other teachers, administrative staff, and parents who want to know what is going on that day and whether the objective has been clearly communicated to the students.

One of the benefits of a clearly written, focused objective is that the teacher knows exactly what to evaluate – did the students learn the objective for the day? Another benefit is that the evaluation works in reverse also – providing a measure for the teacher to judge his/her own effectiveness. It is the primary purpose of an objective to focus the students on what they are to learn that day; in addition, a well-written objective might also motivate students to want to learn the day's lesson.

18: Answer = A. This objective is generic enough to emphasize knowledge and skills that would apply in a variety of situations – knowledge about science fiction and fantasy helps to evaluate a large number of reading selections.

The content of an objective should be specific enough that anyone reading it will understand the subject matter. The content should be able to stand alone and be understood without having to look up specific materials; consequently, answer B is not a good example of content because it refers to specific materials -- Unit 6 in the vocabulary book. In like manner, answer D refers to specific materials (p. 114 in the textbook). The content should also be generic enough that the emphasis is on knowledge and skills that are applicable in a number of contexts; answer C is not generic enough but could be fixed by adding the skills that would be learned from the task.

19: Answer = B. "Know" might be appropriate for a general goal or standard, but is not a measurable action. The teacher cannot know if a student truly comprehends or has learned something unless there is a demonstration of the knowledge.

The behavior component of an objective states what students will do to demonstrate their learning. Thus, this component is written as an observable verb so that the outcome can be measured. Calculate, define, and predict all ask the students to do a specific, concrete task, probably written. These verbs command an action.

20: Answer = C. This response describes the learning condition rather than the evaluation condition. Objectives focus on outcomes, not on when or where the students gain the knowledge; therefore, "after completing the unit on World War I" is not a good example of an evaluation condition.

Describing the evaluation condition or conditions of an objective provides additional specificity about what the student will learn. The condition can affect the difficulty level of the objective and determine the lesson and practice activities. An evaluation condition should ask students to perform a skill in isolation or in context, tell students what information or materials will be provided, or describe the setting or situation involved in the objective. Answer A is an example of materials provided – on graph paper. Answer B is an example of a setting or situation – during partner practice. Answer D is an example of information provided – given a list of European countries.

21: Answer = A. Objectives are intended to communicate clearly with students, parents, and other professionals, but "as assessed by the teacher" is not a valid criterion for acceptable performance because that leaves the objective open to interpretation.

The criterion component of an objective specifies the standard of acceptable performance; that is, how well the student must do to meet the objective. Examples of criterion include demonstration of knowledge as a total number or proportion, in terms of time, as a variation, as a description or result, or a combination of these. Answer B, "with no errors," gives the total number of acceptable errors. Answer C sets the criterion in terms of time: "for ten minutes each day." Answer D describes the criterion as a variation: "to the nearest whole number" (as opposed to the nearest tenth or hundredth).

22: Answer = D. Setting an objective without a specific time or amount limit would leave students wondering if there will ever be an end to the task.

A common error when writing a criterion is to set it too low, so answer A would be the correct way to write a criterion: setting performance standards high enough to meet skills expectations, especially in reading, writing, and math. Another common error is to set the criterion arbitrarily; for example, setting the accuracy rate for 80% every time, no matter the difficulty of the task, or asking that a task be performed in too short a time. Answer B is correct in directing that the teacher set realistic standards and time limits. Answer C is also a correct way to set the criterion at the right level, gradually increasing expectations for accuracy in a skill; for example, 50% by October, 65% by November, and so on.

23: Answer = C. The purpose of an objective is to represent important learning outcomes.

Answer A is incorrect because objectives should be written to describe outcomes, not activities or assignments. Answer B is incorrect because objectives should be clean and simple for clarity, not creative or complex and thus ripe for confusion. Answer D is incorrect because objectives can be well written in terms of form but still manage to be inappropriate for the students.

24: Answer = D. Although copying definitions might help to cement the meaning of a word, if the word is not one that is relevant to the lesson, it will be quickly forgotten. Answer D violates the guideline that practicing skills should be embedded within application opportunities and is busy-work practice with no point to the effort.

Reading does help students to improve word attack skills, as well as many other skills, so Answer A is a worthwhile objective. If the objective is to improve number facts and computations, solving problems is a good practice, so Answer B is also a worthwhile objective. In the process of writing an essay, the student has to practice spelling and penmanship skills, so this assignment achieves a good objective, as stated in Answer C.

25: Answer = C. Memorizing dates is a low-level skill that does not require any analysis or comprehension; thus the task in Answer C is not a higher-level objective.

Making predictions involves sufficient comprehension of the information given to be able to make an extension from it; this is a higher-level thinking skill and Answer A is a higher-level objective. Suggesting courses of action is also an extension of the given information and requires higher-level thinking to create a plan; thus Answer B is a higher-level objective. Similarly, providing solutions to problems involves critical thinking skills, so Answer D is a higher-level objective.

26: Answer = B. An advantage of doing objectives is that, if done properly, the exercise will cause the teacher to think about skills that the students need to learn.

Answer A states an obvious problem: teachers are not supposed to be aiming for low-level skills in an objective, even if such skills are easily measurable. Answer C is a common problem: teachers in effect write the same objective day after day because they get in a rut, and it's easy to use the same pattern again and again rather than think through what objective best fits the lesson. Answer D is a problem if the teacher is so focused on the objective of the day that s/he forgets that it is supposed to fit into the big picture of the course or unit.

27: Answer = C. Task cards are a strategy best used as a manipulative for tactile-kinesthetic learners. While a task card may have writing on it, the value to tactile learners is that a card is something that the students can touch, which makes the writing more real to them.

Students who are dominantly verbal-linguistic learners will learn best when listening, speaking, reading, and writing. Consequently, activities such as classroom discussions, listening to a story read by the teacher, or reading the words listed on the classroom word wall are good strategies for reaching the verbal-linguistic learners in the class.

28: Answer = A. Conducting interviews is a strategy best used for verbal-linguistic students who use speaking, such as asking questions of another person, to learn.

Students who are dominantly logical-mathematical learners will learn best in the areas of mathematics, science, and logic. Strategies in these areas include using Venn diagrams to logically illustrate relationships; thinking in probabilities, which emphasizes working with numbers; and discerning patterns, which is a mathematical thinking process.

29: Answer = B. Syllogisms are a method of diagramming logical thought, a strategy that would work best with a logical-mathematical learner.

Students who are dominantly tactile-kinesthetic learners will learn best when they can use their bodies or parts of their bodies, such as hands, to solve problems. Consequently, strategies such as large-floor games (those that require bodily movement over an area), dance warm-ups (also involving bodily movement), and role-playing, which allows the use of drama to illustrate a lesson, are good strategies for reaching the tactile-kinesthetic learners in the class.

30: Answer = A. A student who enjoys building models is most likely a tactile-kinesthetic learner who enjoys hands-on activities; that is, activities that allow the student to create and learn while touching related materials.

Teachers discern the learning styles of students through testing or observation. A student who easily perceives patterns and relationships is likely a logical-mathematical learner. A student who listens and responds to the spoken work or who is interested in writing is likely a verbal-linguistic learner.

31:Answer = C. The ability to learn languages with relative ease is a characteristic of the verbal-linguistic learner.

Teachers discern the learning styles of students through testing or observation. A student who likes field trips and physical exercise is likely a tactile-kinesthetic learner who enjoys the physical activity of a field trip or any physical exercise because such a student learns through involvement of the body. Similarly, a tactile-kinesthetic learner will exhibit greater skill with balance and dexterity. A student who is good at logical problem solving is likely a logical-mathematical learner.

32: Answer = C. A logical-mathematical learner is most likely to be interested in a career in engineering, which involves mathematics and logical problem solving.

Teachers discern the learning styles of students through testing or observation. A student who is sensitive to physical environments and systems or who is interested in a career as a builder is a tactile-kinesthetic learner since these involve the use of the body in the learning/practicing process. A student who reads, speaks, and writes effectively is a verbal-linguistic learner who excels at tasks using the spoken or written word.

33: Answer = C. A student who enjoys playing with sound is most likely a musical learner who learns best when the material has rhythm and melody.

Teachers discern the learning styles of students through testing or observation. A student who uses clustering as a brainstorming tool (which allows visualization of the ideas), highlights reading materials in color (which visually emphasizes important information), or uses visual memory techniques is a visual-spatial learner.

34: Answer = D. A student who responds well to materials of varying shapes is a visual-spatial learner who remembers items according to their shapes, who learns by seeing and observing, not listening to music.

Teachers discern the learning styles of students through testing or observation. A student who listens and responds with interest to a variety of sounds, wants to learn to sing or play an instrument, or wants to be a sound engineer is most likely a musical learner who responds to rhythm and melody.

35: Answer = C. The library is the answer because reading requires the kind of quiet that allows the reader to become absorbed in the book. Classically, libraries are quiet places and that applies to a classroom library area as well.

Children need space for art work, but not necessarily a quiet area. Science activities, since they are activities, can be noisy anyway, so a quiet area is not critical. A puppet stage is likely to produce laughter and applause, so such a noisy activity does not require a quiet area.

36: Answer = D. The answer is all of the above, because all of the choices describe practical methods of classroom design.

Classrooms with a variety of activity centers need at least one place that is a quiet zone; the way to achieve quiet areas in a classroom is to eliminate distractions and muffle noise with screens, shelves, or other furniture. Children need to feel welcome and comfortable in a classroom, so it is inviting to a child to have the materials they use at eye-level where they can find what they need and reach it. Children also, however, need to understand that the classroom is a place to learn and not to roughhouse, so the classroom should be designed with traffic patterns that do not have long open stretches that would tempt children to run.

37: Answer = A. Making labels in more than one language is not confusing to the children. Rather, it is supportive of their home language (if it is not English), and bi-lingual or multi-lingual labels send the message that writing comes in a variety of shapes and languages.

A print-rich environment includes labels to identify objects and work areas, print that is at a child's eye level so it can be seen easily, and print that was created by the children themselves so that they can make the connection between print and their own work. That connection between individual creation and print is reinforced when the teacher models writing by preparing posters and other written materials in front of the children.

38: Answer = C. The message will not be that the work is more important than rules and tidiness, but will be that anything goes, or that neither the teacher nor the students need care about order and cleanliness.

A classroom needs to look neat and organized to show that the teacher cares and has good management. A messy or poorly organized classroom has a sense of chaos that causes disruptive behavior, especially when children are frustrated by not being able to find what they need or not having sufficient room to work. Children have difficulty choosing activities if the materials are in disarray such that they can't find all the pieces or can't clearly see what is available when the choices are piled together. If the classroom is already messy, how are children to know if they were successful at their clean-up chores or understand the need if the teacher has demonstrated a lack of concern about clean up and organization.

39: Answer = B. Labels make it easier for children to find things on their own and put them away correctly; that is, children are more independent and responsible when they can follow the labels by themselves. Labels are not a crutch that relieves children of responsibility; reading a label or icon is empowering and asks the children to follow instructions.

Placing labels on as many items as possible in the classroom has the benefit of teaching the children systems of organization and storage; children learn sorting and putting things in their place so that they can be easily found when needed again. Such organization enhances the sense of structure and security for children. Labels, as print materials, naturally add to the print-rich environment of the classroom and impress the children with the value of print. Further, labels help children to associate words with actual objects, thus connecting the abstract with the concrete.

40: Answer = B. While setting rules and establishing routines is important to classroom management, the teacher should not be so firm that there is no room for flexibility and adjustments.

A teacher's relationship with a child must remain consistent in terms of the teacher's interactions with the child and the expectations set for the child; a moody or fickle teacher can frustrate and anger the children. Teachers should respond to children positively and avoid negativity for the relationship to be constructive and nurturing. Although the teacher is the ultimate decision-maker in the classroom and must establish authority, sharing power with the children by guiding them into making responsible choices gives the children a sense of empowerment and a stake in the classroom situation.

41: Answer = B. There should be follow-up to the conflict resolution to make certain that the children are sticking to their agreed-upon solution and to ensure that the conflict does not re-occur. Some teachers might feel that dropping the issue will help everyone forget the conflict, but that usually is not the case.

Conflicts are best handled with calmness and a quiet voice as the teacher gathers information about the conflict in order to get a complete and fair picture of the situation. Then the teacher should review the conflict with the children and ask for their ideas for ways the problem could have been prevented and ways to solve the conflict. Involving the children in the resolution of the problem teaches them self-regulation and respect for themselves and others.

42: Answer = D. All of the responses demonstrate that clear and immediate communication is the best way to deal with children with behavioral problems.

Children with behavioral problems are best managed with clear, distinct communication. Therefore, potentially vague instructions must be revised prior to presentation to be as explicit as possible so the child cannot claim to have misunderstood or argue that the teacher said something else. This type of students does best when there is not a gap of time between instructions and practice, but rather by immediate involvement in the activity while the child still remembers what to do and has not yet had a chance to get distracted.

The same sense of immediacy is needed for feedback or the student will not be able to connect the feedback to the activity.

43: Answer = C. Clear communication is always best for effective classroom management, especially when instructions and expectations are delineated before the lesson starts.

Saying that a reward will be given "if everyone does well" is too vague and sets up conflicts. Rewards, like assessments, should be dependent on individual effort, generally. Younger children do not usually have the focus or sense of time to be able to wait for an award for a week, or to associate an award with the action that earned the reward over a week's time. Awards should be given as close to the lesson or activity for which the reward was offered as possible. "Customizing" consequences for misbehavior would be exhausting for the teacher, confusing for the children, and at risk of being interpreted as favoritism or discrimination.

44: Answer = C. The teacher should anticipate problems and be prepared with appropriate reactions rather than trying to think of what to do on the spot. Teachers need to be flexible, and unexpected things will happen, but the wise teacher will try to anticipate behavioral problems that might result from a changed situation.

Stepping outside the classroom routine for special activities can result in chaos unless the teacher anticipates problems and plans for additional behavior management specific to the new situation. This planning should include how to re-arrange the seats so that the activity can proceed with sufficient space and accommodate groups or partners if needed; selecting the partners so that teams work well together; and reinforcing the rules with strong reminders of consequences.

45: Answer = D. The answer is all of the above because all of the situations described required additional pre-planning for the teacher.

The types of lessons that call for additional behavior management include: 1) ones that will have multiple steps and transitions because each transition is an opportunity for students to get off task; 2) ones that will require lots of equipment because the teacher will be distracted while using the equipment or the students will be excited and lack patience when trying to use new equipment; 3) ones that require additional and unusual materials that will have to be distributed because children will again be eager to receive the materials and start trying them out.

46: Answer = D. Peer helpers are more likely to keep the restless student on task than to distract that student; therefore, peer helpers are a good idea.

Allowing a student who has trouble staying on task to do a "gallery walk"; that is, to expend some energy by walking around to examine the lesson materials that are on display, is a good practice because once the student has seen the materials s/he is less likely to be distracted by wondering about them. A student who has trouble staying on task is helped by being assigned specific tasks to accomplish because breaking up the assignment into smaller jobs seems more achievable. Using response cards catches the attention of the student who has trouble staying on task and pulls that student into the lesson with the others.

47: Answer = A. The students always need to see the teacher as well as whatever is pertinent to the lesson around the room.

No matter the activity or room arrangement, the teacher always needs to be able to get close to each student so that the teacher can give assistance wherever necessary. Small group work, individual work, or discussions may need furniture rearrangement to best facilitate the activity, so it is standard practice to move desks and tables around to suit the lesson. When students work in pairs or teams, it is important that the teacher selects the pairs or teams to ensure compatibility and good work while avoiding problems that might result from conflicts between students or good friends sitting next to each other and being more interested in personal matters than the lesson.

48: Answer = B. The routine clean-up process may not be sufficient if extra materials or messy substances such as glue or paint have been used. Effective time management would include anticipation of the need for additional clean-up instruction and time; otherwise, students might rush or leave a mess when the routine proves insufficient for the task. Teachers shouldn't assume that the students know what to do for clean up when the situation changes.

Total preparation means checking out the equipment prior to classroom use to avoid problems, having all the supplies ready so there are no delays while supplies are hunted for or pulled out of cabinets, and giving lesson-specific instructions about sharing and returning materials prior to students jumping into the lesson so that the activity does not have to be interrupted for corrective instruction or additional information.

49: Answer = D. The answer is all of the above because the A, B, and C choices are all standard to setting up routines in the classroom.

A teacher who has good classroom-management skills will have certain routines in place that establish order and discipline. Among these are set routines for handing in assignments (for example, placing homework in a certain tray); for what a student should do upon completing a task (for example, take out something to read, rest head on desk, wait quietly); and for how to set up desks for partner practice (for example, turning the desks toward each other and dividing the materials). In each situation, the student knows exactly what to do and there are no questions or fussing about the steps.

50: Answer = C. While the command doesn't use "don't" or "no," it brings up a negative scenario: "fighting." It would be better to say something like "Let's share the crayons."

The word "not" is a negative and some teachers find themselves saying "Don't do that"; "Don't talk"; and so forth all day long. The teacher needs to make an effort to eliminate "not," "no" and wording that indicates negatives from their commands and comments. Answer A is a good alternative to "Don't slam the door." Answer B is a positive alternative to "Don't copy." Answer D is a positive alternative to "Don't guess" and encourages critical thinking.

51: Answer = B. Students prefer private, quietly delivered praise. This way they get the praise they want, but they are not embarrassed by anything dramatic or un-cool.

Answer A is incorrect because students are often embarrassed by loud praise; they don't want to stand out. Answer C is incorrect because it's not cool to be too goodie-goodie, so they don't want to be pointed out for good behavior. Answer D is incorrect because, although teachers want to give credit to students for their effort, praising work that is poor sends a confusing message to the student that poor work is acceptable; the teacher needs to communicate clearly that the effort was good, but the work still did not meet standards.

52: Answer = A. Making a big deal out of praise does not necessarily make a student feel special. Instead, it might embarrass the student with too much "gushing" that seems overdone.

Answer B is a good guideline for communicating praise because being specific lets the student know exactly what s/he did correctly and will therefore be able to repeat the correct action rather than wonder what was good about the product because of vague praise. Answer C is also a good guideline for communicating praise because praise isn't convincing if the teacher does not match the words with appropriate body language and tone of voice. Answer D refers to specificity of praise again and reminds the teacher to look for opportunities for praise as in new skills or evidence of progress.

53: Answer = D. The answer is all of the above because all of the strategies are effective.

It is good for the teacher to give examples of success from former students of the school because current students can best identify with those who have been where they are, so answer A is encouraging information to communicate.   Although some teachers try to avoid letting students know any personal information, students find examples from the teachers' lives to be really interesting. In the case of sharing about how one can apply what was learned in school, it is a good idea for teachers to give personal examples as recommended in answer B. Just as commercials use celebrities to endorse products, so teachers can use examples from celebrities to endorse the benefits of school; answer C is a good technique for communicating the link between school and real life.

54: Answer = B. The answer uses a negative and is just like saying, "Eat your spinach because it is good for you." Kids want to do what they like, not necessarily what's good for them.

Answer A is a positive communication that creates anticipation for learning because the teacher is setting expectations and giving students a goal for achieving a skill that might be interesting. Answer C sets up an expectation of curiosity that encourages students to want to find out more. Answer D is another way that a teacher can interest students who have a curiosity about the teacher's personal life, and is very inviting because it offers to share something with the students.

55: Answer = A. Words like "because" and "for example" have to be followed by a reasonably precise explanation that gives clarity to the communication.

Clarity is critical to good communication. Vague or confusing language can reduce the effectiveness of presentations. Answer B gives examples of negated intensifiers; that is, the use of words such as "many" and "very" that indicate something big, but that are qualified by a "not", which communicates a nebulous state. Answer C indicates an ambiguous designation or destination – how is the student supposed to figure out needed specific information, even how to find supplies in the closet, if the directions are so vague? Answer D has words with the problem of vague probability; the student doesn't know exactly how often or what percentage.

56: Answer = B. If the 5th graders are doing less demanding work than the 3rd graders, then communication has broken down among the teachers or between the principal and teachers about the level of work that is expected of all students at that school. Students and parents alike will be wondering why the 5th graders are not being expected to do more than 3rd graders as evidence of their skills and knowledge progress.

Answer A indicates effective communication if the students know the lesson's objective; such knowledge is required for good teaching. Answer C indicates that the 5th grade teachers have communicated effectively with each other and are working as a team for organized instruction. Answer D describes a situation that is good practice for communicating to students the expectations and standards of an assignment.

57: Answer = D. The answer is all of the above, because all of the options are advantages of using a series of graphics to enhance a lesson.

Using a series of graphics, i.e., pictures or icons, is a good way to assist visual learners with knowledge retention. Having students make their own copies of these graphics provides kinesthetic learners with a hands-on activity to aid their learning. When the graphics are in a certain order, students are better able to understand a series of events or how the elements of the lesson are linked. Graphics also provide a concrete representation of any abstract concepts in the lesson, which clarifies the lesson for students.

58: Answer = C. The one activity that is not a good continuation of the graphics lesson would be to grade the students on the quality of their artwork in reproducing the graphics. The lesson is not about art, so the students should not be graded on their artistic skills. Doing so would only penalize those students who are not artistically inclined on a lesson where they otherwise might have success.

The graphics series can be beneficial in follow-up exercises, such as using the graphics to review as well as teach the lesson. If it is important for the students to learn the order in which the graphics appear, then the teacher can make sets of the graphics, divide the class into teams, then give one set to each team of students who will then compete to see which team can put the graphics in order in the fastest time.

59: Answer = B. Allowing students to pick their own groups defeats the purposes outlined above and will most likely result in groups that were chosen by the students so that they could be with friends rather than good working partners.

Flexible grouping is designed to put students together in groups that work well for various purposes. One type of group would be one in which the students can work according to similar interests. Others would group students according to readiness levels or specific skill levels. In other words, the grouping would be teacher-selected according to assessments that indicate the needed diversity or similarities to make the group efficient.

60: Answer = A. Experience shows that the practice does not grow old but remains an effective tool that the students enjoy using because it is quick, active, and does not involve individual pressures.

Using response cards involves all of the students at the same time, so students who might otherwise daydream or be reluctant to give an answer are swept up into the activity; they have less fear of answering when part of a group and can't easily go off task when everyone around is engaged. Using response cards for just 30 minutes per day instead of hand raising elicits more than 3,700 additional academic responses during the school year (Harvard et al., 1996), so it is a highly effective method for engaging students in lessons. Using response cards also allows teachers to assess student understanding of the lesson in a glance.

61: Answer = C. As an assessment tool that checks individual responses, using response cards is not designed for group or pair work where a stronger student might be able to pick the answers for a weaker student who would then not be identified for remediation.

Using response cards actively engages students in an assessment since they must make a choice and physically raise a card. The strategy is one that can be used as a pre-assessment before a lesson that might also attract student interest in the upcoming lesson. The strategy can also be used during the lesson to check understanding and progress, and of course, after the lesson as a quick assessment of mastery. As an assessment tool, using response cards, perhaps in shorter question sets, enables teachers to find the areas that need re-teaching.

62: Answer = D. The answer is all of the above because all of the first three strategies are legitimate.

A student who can disappear in the crowd of a classroom is more likely to wander off task; however, a student who is given preferential seating at a desk near the teacher or other adult, or with a group of quiet students, or away from high traffic areas, or at a desk alone rather than at a table with other students will be more likely to keep his/her attention on the subject. Sometimes, a student who is easily distracted needs to be placed in a study carrel where visual distractions can be minimized. Another strategy for reducing distractions is to eliminate sounds through the use of headphones – the student hears only the lesson, not all the other noises in the classroom.

63: Answer = B. It helps students to stick to a task if the task is made more fun by adding novelty to it through games or personal interest materials.

For students who have difficulty staying with and completing routine tasks, the teacher can employ certain strategies that will encourage the child to stick with the work. One way is to explain to the students about the importance of remaining on-task and monitoring oneself. Another way is to eliminate any part of the routine that really isn't necessary, such as copying sentences. Still another way is to break up the task into smaller time commitments. In this way, the student doesn't get too bored before being allowed to go to something else, but is nonetheless required to come back in a timely manner to finish.

64: Answer = A. One has to have the regular routine first, and then one can have remedial strategies for breaks in the routine.

Some students, especially the youngest students, have difficulty coping with change; they need the stability of routine and find deviations from the norm to be threatening or frightening. The primary strategy for dealing with this situation is to maintain the posted schedule as much as possible. When visitors or special events do occur, it helps, of course, to prepare the students by telling them in advance of the change in schedule, Those children who are still disturbed by the change can be helped by being near someone they trust during the visit or activity. The teacher can even teach relaxation techniques to the students and suggest these techniques when a student appears to be having anxiety over a change in routine.

65: Answer = C. The best approach for a teacher in regards to using technology in the classroom is to use only the technology with which s/he is comfortable so that the technology does not complicate or distract from the lesson.

Answer A is not the best approach because while the teacher should know enough to demonstrate the technology used in the classroom, it is not the teacher's job to teach technology; therefore, the teacher should not be hesitant to use technology out of fear of having to become a technical expert. Answer B is not the best approach because the teacher needs to find a balance between using the technology center and working with computers in the classroom. It is more convenient to stay in the classroom, but the technology center exists to expand capabilities. Answer D is not the best approach because while increasing technology might improve instruction, there is no guarantee; only better teaching can improve instruction.

66: Answer = D. The answer is all of the above because all of the statements about the benefits of student computer use for compositions are true.

Answer A is true because students do not have to worry about penmanship and neatness when writing on a computer, so they find the product more attractive and likely to get a better grade. Answer B is true because the students don't have to worry about their spelling, or grammar for that matter, if they use the spelling and grammar checks. This means that they can relax and concentrate on the content itself. Answer C is true because the cut-and-paste feature of the word processor allows for easy reorganizing and rewriting, which saves time and energy.

67: Answer = A. The research shows that instruction and student progress are greatly aided by the use of computers. Some states actually forbid the use of computers in certain areas because computers can't be used on the state test, but this prohibition ignores the benefits of computer instruction and the ability of students to transition to testing without computers.

Many teachers have serious trepidations about using computers in the classroom. When trying to figure out whether they can handle the technology or whether there will be sufficient benefit from using computers, teachers should ask if the software is complicated and boring or easy to use and fun for the students. Teachers should also ask whether there will be sufficient technological support if anything should go wrong. If the teacher is software and hardware with insufficient technical support, h/she runs the risk of having the software running on only a few computers, or multiple computers not working properly. Teachers should be concerned about the effect of computers on student behavior; on this issue they should be reassured that student behavior is generally better when students, who love technology, can be engaged by a computer.

68: Answer = D. The answer is all of the above, because all of the statements in A, B, and C are issues that should be considered when doing research, and all students should be taught these precautions about reliable sources.

Considering the unreliability of some web sites, students should be cautioned, as mentioned in answer A, to find several information sources with different perspectives as a way to get a balanced view of the issue being researched; phony web sites should become obvious by comparison. Answer B gives advice about another way to check the credibility of a web site by making sure the web site has an identified author or institutional sponsor; if whoever is behind the web site is unidentified, the web site is suspicious. Answer C advises students to check for the latest date of update; if the last time the site was updated is years ago, then the information could be out-of-date.

69: Answer = A. Despite the large number of federal and state grants to help schools with high poverty and minority populations to catch up with schools in higher socio-economic areas, the poorer schools still lag behind in technology.

Answer B is a true statement about the limitations placed on the teacher and students if there are not enough computers available for use in the classroom; not much more can be done than demonstrations and the occasional individual work. Answer C is true in that having more than two computers in the classroom allows more student access for collaboratives; allows more time on computers for students since they don't have to share as much; and enables students to work on more complex projects, such as research and portfolios. Answer D is true and very important to know; while we assume that all kids are fans of technology, that does not mean that they have access to technology at home, and the income level for having a home computer is perhaps surprisingly high.

70: Answer = B. Just as students use group activities as perhaps an antidote to all the time spent alone with technology, students are signing up for extracurricular activities just as much and more than was the norm in pre-computer days.

The answers to this question may be surprising. Although students who have grown up with television, computers, and video games are thereby isolating themselves to activities done alone, answer A is true because, in contrast, they enjoy group activities. Answer C is perhaps obvious because students who dwell on technology love even more new technology. Answer D, that students identify with parents, is true because their toys are not for childhood only but are much the same that the parents use for work and play; technology has brought the worlds of parents and children closer together in daily activities.

71: Answer = C. Technology-loving students find lots of video insets in a presentation engaging and are not confused by them.

Answer A is true because, just as students turn from their technology used alone to do group work or participate in extracurricular activities, students want a break from all that technology on occasion and like to have a plain lecture or discussion. When a written presentation is given by the teacher, such as a PowerPoint, obviously it will be organized more than a verbal presentation, and students like the clarity as stated in answer B. Answer

D is true in that the negative side to a computerized presentation is that the students will just copy the nice, organized notes and not think critically about the content.

72: Answer = A. Somehow students still find time for lots of television while still surfing the Net, participating in chat rooms, and playing video games. The connection is that television is another medium that provides images and entertainment and is, therefore, part of the technology package for students.

It might be easy to assume that technology enthusiasts among students do not watch much television because they are indeed busy surfing the Net (answer B), participating in chat rooms (answer C), and playing lots of video games (answer D).

73: Answer = B. The teacher corrects the student in a nice way by saying "good example," but identifies the form of speech in the mistaken answer and can then go back to the search for an example of a noun.

Answer A would not be appropriate; while the teacher is trying to be nice, to say that a verb could be a noun is misinformation that could confuse students. Answer C is insufficient; the teacher should say nicely, "No, that's a verb. I need a noun." Just saying, "No, I asked for a noun." doesn't let the student know the form of speech for the answer that was given. Answer D is rude and might hurt the student's feelings even if delivered in a teasing manner.

74: Answer = D. Answers A, B, and C are all hallmark ingredients of good feedback.

Answer A is correct in that feedback should contain what the student did right and what the student did wrong. Being clear and specific about what is correct and incorrect helps the student to see the difference. Answer B is correct in that feedback should also contain suggestions for improvement. Examples of situations where there is room for improvement include those in which an answer is correct but does not have an explanation or one that could be extended for more critical thinking. Answer C is correct in that feedback should always end on a positive note; even when the feedback involves correcting a mistake, there are ways to encourage the student to try again or to tell the student that there are signs of improvement.

75: Answer = C. The point is to learn the correct method for the demonstration, not to probe the reasons for the mistake. Questioning the student about the mistake will probably get an "I don't know" response and make the student more nervous from being challenged to explain him or herself.

Answer A is a good suggestion because in the case of a short presentation, it is best to give feedback at the end rather than interrupt the student, which might be upsetting. This is especially true if the feedback involves correcting a mistake. Answer B is a good way to give feedback in a longer presentation that has steps to it because the feedback will then be fresh and pertinent to each step. This is preferable to the student or audience trying to think back in order to connect a step to the feedback. Answer D is a good method for feedback when a step-by-step presentation is given and it is important that the step be done correctly for the rest of the demonstration to work. The teacher should re-demonstrate the step, and then allow the student to try again. It is important to let the student try again; otherwise, the correction will look like teacher interference and the student will not learn how to do the step.

76: Answer = D. Answers A, B, and C are all variations on feedback that give students some independence while allowing the teacher more personal time with those who need intensive assistance.

If the teacher is not available to give feedback, it is acceptable to allow the student to refer to an answer key, as in Answer A. The key provides enough information for the student to know what was correct and what was incorrect and be able to go on from that point; usually in this situation the teacher has established a routine for continuing, depending on the student's score. By allowing students to ask another adult for help, Answer B provides another alternative when the teacher is unavailable to give feedback. Of course, this works only if there is another adult present, but on many activities and exercises, any adult should be able to explain the lesson and interpret the student's results. Answer C, allowing students to work in pairs and critique each other, is a good method of feedback that frees up the teacher's time and often is less stressful for students. Assuming the students are well disciplined, they will enjoy working with each other and often will find it less stressful to make a mistake in front of a classmate than the teacher. This method is best for low-level skills and drills.

77: Answer = B. Although some educators think a long test is too taxing for students and graders, a long test actually gives the students more opportunities to show what they know and gives the teacher more opportunities to cover the entire lesson.

Answer A describes a problem with test making in that uneven sampling of the lesson content can mean that students could study hard in an area where the teacher hardly asks a question. Students feel deceived in such circumstances and it is unfair if students studied, but did not concentrate where the teacher did. Answer C describes a problem with test where all the questions have the same level of difficulty and thus do not challenge the students or provide a way to separate lower and higher achievers. Answer D presents another problem in test making when references or allusions are made to topics unfamiliar to some students; in these cases, the students cannot answer questions because they have not been presented with the information about those topics.

78: Answer = C. While multiple-choice assessment might be intellectually shallower, it can cover more territory than essay questions, which are more focused.

Answer A is not an advantage of multiple-choice tests because, while some information needs to be memorized, critical thinking is even more important and multiple-choice tests do not allow for critical thinking as much as mere memorization. Answer B is not an advantage because, although teachers are always looking for an easy way to do assessment and save time, multiple-choice tests do not necessarily cover the important material as completely as essay tests. Answer D is not an advantage because the nature of a multiple-choice question stem is such that it often can't help but give away the answer to students who are able to deduce or guess well.

79: Answer = A. It is not true that it takes more time to construct short-answer and completion questions than multiple-choice questions; on the contrary, it takes less time to construct the short-answer and completion questions, but probably more time to grade them.

Answer B is true in that short-answer and completion test items are especially useful in math and science because it is necessary to test whether students are able to recall formulas or equations. Answer C is true in that short-answer and completion test items are especially useful for spelling and language courses where specific bits of information often are required in order to do more complex problem-solving tasks. Answer D is true about short-answer and completion test items in that they are like mini-essays and therefore present some of the same scoring problems related to time and subjectivity as essays.

80: Answer = A. One advantage of an essay test or question is that the nature of the answer allows the student to think things through and organize the answer rather than trying to fit into the test form.

Answer B is a disadvantage of essay tests in that grading can be highly subjective and therefore not necessarily consistent or fair. Answer C is a disadvantage of essay tests in that essay questions are focused on a specific area and do not give broad coverage to the material. This specificity reduces the opportunities for a student to do well. Answer D is a disadvantage of essay tests in that good written answers must be organized, legible, and must employ correct spelling and grammar. The advantage in answering essay questions goes to students who are talented in writing and not necessarily to those who have the best answers.

81: Answer = D. This answer reflects the variety of choices.

According to *Home, School, and Community Relations* by Carol Gestwicki, the understanding of the term "parent involvement" is often much narrower than all of the opportunities for involvement that exist. Teachers might think that parent involvement is just keeping parents informed about their student's progress, but it also involves a variety of activities in which parents might engage to assist or improve the school. Therefore, it is important for educators to know a wide variety of ways that parents can be encouraged to undertake involvement. This question addresses the breadth of teachers' knowledge in this area.

82: Answer = C. Participating in an intervention program requires more intense involvement than just a one-time activity such as baking cookies, going on a field trip, or even visiting with the teacher.

Once the educator is aware of the choices for parent involvement, it is also important to understand the difference between high and low levels of involvement. In this manner, parents who are involved only at a low level can be invited to higher levels that will result in a better understanding of the school and classroom situation and thus improve relations between parents and the school. This question tests the educator's understanding of low and high levels of parental involvement.

83: Answer = B. Although a newsletter requires quite a bit of time, it does not involve the parent with the students. Parents sitting in on classes, observing the functions of the school, or actually assisting in the classroom are examples of higher involvement.

Once the educator is aware of the choices for parent involvement, it is also important to understand the difference between high and low levels of involvement. In this manner, parents who are involved only at a low level can be invited to higher levels that will result in a better understanding of the school and classroom situation and thus improve relations between parents and the school. This question tests the educator's understanding of low and high levels of parental involvement.

84: Answer = A. School-based parental education programs are available to parents, but attendance is voluntary, not mandatory. The other choices are all federal programs with mandated parental involvement.

Of the various types of motivation designed to bring about parent involvement in schools, one is legal mandate. It is important for parents and teachers to know that enrollment of a child in certain types of schools requires a commitment from the parents to participate in school matters. This question tests the knowledge of the educator concerning programs that mandate or do not mandate parent involvement. Such knowledge involves an awareness of which programs are government-sponsored and which are not.

85: Answer = C. This choice is a federal program with mandated parental involvement while the other three are non-federal programs that set their own levels of parental involvement.

Of the various types of motivation designed to bring about parent involvement in schools, one is legal mandate. It is important for parents and teachers to know that enrollment of a child in certain types of schools requires a commitment from the parents to participate in school matters. This question tests the knowledge of the educator concerning programs that mandate or do not mandate parent involvement. Such knowledge involves an awareness of which programs are government sponsored and which are not.

86: Answer = B. Socio-economic factors, while important, are still not as important to a child's academic success as quality parental involvement.

Good parenting is so important that all factors directly related to the parent are more important than the effects of the social or economic situation of the family. Even in the midst of poverty and lower-class status, the parent can effectively prepare the child for school and support the child's progress. However, parents need sufficient self-esteem to believe that their contribution is valuable enough to make the effort. With so much emphasis on special strategies for children of poverty, coupled with the emphasis on the effects of poverty, the overriding influence of a parent may be forgotten by educators. Therefore, this question tests the awareness of the educator concerning the critical nature of good parenting.

87: Answer = A. Schools can provide intervention programs to improve parenting skills, but they cannot assume the parenting role in the interim even if it seems that the school is being placed into a position to take that role.

Educators are well aware that schools need to take an active role in community education, as well as that of the children, in order to improve the abilities of the parents to successfully promote the academic progress of their children. Schools partner with other agencies to assist in the delivery of needed services, attempt to involve the parent in the child's education, and offer to be an extension of the family in the academic setting. However, the interaction does not extend to actually usurping the authority of the parents, even when the parents have poor parenting skills.

88: Answer = D. A, B, and C are all effective methods for overcoming difficulties with interacting with parents.

Teachers get into the business of teaching to work with children, not parents. Consequently, some may feel very ill at ease with parents or see parents as interfering with their classrooms. Some teachers may be fine with children, but timid around adults. To remedy this problem, it is helpful for these teachers to prepare their comments and set an agenda in advance of a parent meeting, so that the teacher has more confidence and is less likely to say something unintended. It is also helpful for teachers to share their concerns, learn from the experience of others, and find out that other teachers share the same fears. It is also good personal discipline and helpful to classroom management if teachers set goals on reaching a certain number of parents each week. This goal setting pressures the teacher into completing calls when they are reluctant to make contact.

89: Answer = C. Although teachers can pick up good tips from each other, too often the lounge is the place where teachers go to gripe and hide instead of sharing and collaborating.

Answer A is an acceptable way to pursue professional development. The tapes and videos are there for the teachers' benefit and can be an effective means of learning. Answer B is an excellent method of maintaining knowledge in the field; subscribing to an education journal should be a given for any teacher. Answer D is obviously a good way to improve teacher performance since conferences, seminars, and workshops are designed for that purpose.

90: Answer = D. The answer is all of the above, because those who provide professional development need to make sure that it covers not only content, but also overall teaching skills in a way that is stimulating and helpful to the teachers.

Answer A refers to the type of professional development that is specific to content knowledge. Deepening and broadening content knowledge enables teachers to better transmit the content to the students. Answer B refers to the type of professional development that focuses on the teaching and learning process in general and refreshes the skills of the teachers. Answer C refers to the way professional development should be delivered so that the teachers are intellectually engaged and aided in their quest for solutions to the complexities of teaching.

91: Answer = B. Although pay incentives certainly encourage teachers to pursue professional development, teachers do not have to be given extra pay to attend, and should not need pay incentives to want to further their teacher education.

Answer A lists a critical need of teachers when it comes to professional development: time. With all their duties and the requirements of the teaching calendar, it is very difficult to find time for professional development. Answer C, support, is necessary for teachers to be able to participate in professional development – support from administrators, fellow teachers, and parents. Answer D is an important aspect of professional development because, even when teachers can find the time, they need the monetary resources to attend and then the resources of supplies and materials to follow up on their training.

92: Answer = D. Professional development is not a trickle-down process but rather a collaboration of experts and teachers sharing research and experience.

Answer A is not true because, although some principles of teaching are universal, a priority of professional development is to help the teachers where they are in order to help with site-specific needs. Answer B is not true because, although some professional development might be about classroom strategies, other types of professional development are definitely aimed at improving content knowledge. Answer C is not true because, like Answer A, although teachers should be aware of other opportunities in the field of education, a priority of professional development is to help the teacher with the job at hand.

93: Answer = A. Although answers B, C, and D are all challenging tasks of professional development, studies show that the biggest challenge is finding the time in the crowded school calendar to present the information and do follow-up.

Answer B is certainly a challenge in that the development of seminars to teach how to implement new educational standards is often complex and limited by time restraints, but this challenge is just part of the business of professional development. Answer C is a challenge because addressing any form of change requires developing adequate explanations and demonstrating how to implement the changes, often while meeting resistance from the constituent audience. Answer D is a challenge because it involves intensive research into the diverse populations and figuring out best practices.

94: Answer = D. Involving parents in planning professional development is a good way to make them a part of the school community and strengthen understanding of the goals of the school. It is the best of the choices for this question.

Answer A is not a good way to conduct professional development because administrators should be involved in and supportive of team planning and all other aspects of teacher collaboration, not off to the side acting like a separate unit. Answer B is an acceptable way of doing professional development because it takes advantage of the teacher's free time and allows for more extended courses; however, summer professional development means that the teachers have to give up their vacation time and will not be able to immediately apply what they have learned in the classroom, which might mean a loss of momentum. Answer C is done occasionally, but removing a whole group of teachers from the school is disruptive and the quality of instruction might suffer with substitutes.

95: Answer = C. Although distance education may be more convenient, it is very important for teachers to collaborate with other teachers, to be involved in their school community, and to enjoy the social aspect of meeting with other teachers and educational professionals. Hiding out at home with the computer is not the best way to pursue professional development.

Answer A is a good way to get professional development through technology because video conferences online are just as professionally prepared and have just as important topics as live seminars. Answer B is a good way to get professional development because exchanging information with other teachers is a valid method for educating oneself about content or best practices. Answer D is a good way to get professional development because, like Answer B, networking with other teachers is an excellent source of information.

96: Answer = C. What is true is not that teachers should spend less time or only their own time for professional development, but that teachers should actually spend more time--at least 20% of their work time--in professional study and collaborative work. Professional development is an essential part of teaching and it is, therefore, legitimate to provide professional development opportunities during work time. Furthermore, it is also reasonable to expect teachers to incorporate continuous learning for themselves during the school day.

Answer A is what some critics of time spent on professional development say, but it shows a lack of understanding of the complexity and needs of the classroom teacher. Answer B is also a common comment of critics of the educational system, but this criticism does not exhibit an understanding of the changes in education that require teachers to need education themselves in order to keep up. Answer D is another common complaint from people who resent teachers being out of the classroom for professional development. Such complaints show a lack of understanding about the need for extensive, continuous professional development and a failure to recognize that time restraints might require taking teachers out of the classroom to accommodate the requirement.

97: Answer = C. While many laws are based on ethics, not all laws are ethical. Examples of unethical laws include the Jim Crow laws in the United States that restricted the civil rights of black people, or laws such as those imposed in Nazi Germany that permitted taking the lives and property of Jews.

Answer A is correct in that laws are written and therefore are not just ideas but are concrete and enacted by people of authority. Answer B is correct in that ethics are a personal code enforced by a person's own conscience; they are not written down but are ideas. Answer D is correct in that society transfers many of its ethics into laws to codify them.

98: Answer = C. If Betty is an ethical person, she will not consider trying to avoid her responsibilities in the situation. Ignoring a problem and hoping it will go away or passing off a problem to someone else is not ethical behavior.

Answer A is a consideration in that Betty's ethics include sympathy for someone needing a job; Betty does not want to cause hardship to another person. Answer B is a consideration in that Betty has an ethical responsibility to comply with the principal's request. Answer D is a consideration in that Betty's ethics dictate that the students should come first; therefore, she needs to make sure they have a competent teacher.

99: Answer = D. The answer is all of the above because Answers A, B, and C are all everyday ways that teachers can ethically influence students.

Answer A is an everyday way that teachers can ethically influence students. Teachers are tightly restricted on what they can convey to students and are thus warned to stay away from anything potentially controversial, but setting a good example in terms of a work ethic and a caring personality are certainly acceptable as ethics to be passed on to students. Answer B, establishing a classroom climate of respect and cooperation, is not only an acceptable means of transmitting ethics; such an environment is essential for good teaching. Answer C is an everyday way that teachers can share ethical values with their students, and have students share those values among themselves. To accomplish this sharing, however, the teacher must ensure that the classroom discussion of ethics stays on the subject matter of the lesson and does not result in anyone trying to force any particular viewpoint on others.

100: Answer = B. A school district does not have to justify its reasons for not rehiring a teacher who is on probation, as unfair as that might seem, and it is clearly specified in a probationary contract that the teacher can be dismissed without reason.

Answer A is a correct statement because it is a requirement that dismissal hearings be scheduled at a reasonable time and place to avoid unfair treatment. Answer C is a correct statement because, at a dismissal hearing, due process requires that the defendant be able to confront and question witnesses so that both sides are heard. Answer D is a correct statement in that the teacher must be given sufficient time to prepare a proper defense and possibly hire an attorney. Additionally, the teacher must be provided with details about the reasons for dismissal in order to know what to address at the hearing. Denying sufficient time and information to prepare a defense would be unfair.

Secret Key #1 - Time is Your Greatest Enemy

Pace Yourself

Wear a watch. At the beginning of the test, check the time (or start a chronometer on your watch to count the minutes), and check the time after every few questions to make sure you are "on schedule."

If you are forced to speed up, do it efficiently. Usually one or more answer choices can be eliminated without too much difficulty. Above all, don't panic. Don't speed up and just begin guessing at random choices. By pacing yourself, and continually monitoring your progress against your watch, you will always know exactly how far ahead or behind you are with your available time. If you find that you are one minute behind on the test, don't skip one question without spending any time on it, just to catch back up. Take 15 fewer seconds on the next four questions, and after four questions you'll have caught back up. Once you catch back up, you can continue working each problem at your normal pace.

Furthermore, don't dwell on the problems that you were rushed on. If a problem was taking up too much time and you made a hurried guess, it must be difficult. The difficult questions are the ones you are most likely to miss anyway, so it isn't a big loss. It is better to end with more time than you need than to run out of time.

Lastly, sometimes it is beneficial to slow down if you are constantly getting ahead of time. You are always more likely to catch a careless mistake by working more slowly than quickly, and among very high-scoring test takers (those who are likely to have lots of time left over), careless errors affect the score more than mastery of material.

Secret Key #2 - Guessing is not Guesswork

You probably know that guessing is a good idea - unlike other standardized tests, there is no penalty for getting a wrong answer. Even if you have no idea about a question, you still have a 20-25% chance of getting it right.

Most test takers do not understand the impact that proper guessing can have on their score. Unless you score extremely high, guessing will significantly contribute to your final score.

Monkeys Take the Test

What most test takers don't realize is that to insure that 20-25% chance, you have to guess randomly. If you put 20 monkeys in a room to take this test, assuming they answered once per question and behaved themselves, on average they would get 20-25% of the questions correct. Put 20 test takers in the room, and the average will be much lower among guessed questions. Why?

1. The test writers intentionally write deceptive answer choices that "look" right. A test taker has no idea about a question, so picks the "best looking" answer, which is often wrong. The monkey has no idea what looks good and what doesn't, so will consistently be lucky about 20-25% of the time.
2. Test takers will eliminate answer choices from the guessing pool

based on a hunch or intuition. Simple but correct answers often get excluded, leaving a 0% chance of being correct. The monkey has no clue, and often gets lucky with the best choice.

This is why the process of elimination endorsed by most test courses is flawed and detrimental to your performance- test takers don't guess, they make an ignorant stab in the dark that is usually worse than random.

$5 Challenge

Let me introduce one of the most valuable ideas of this course- the $5 challenge:

You only mark your "best guess" if you are willing to bet $5 on it.
You only eliminate choices from guessing if you are willing to bet $5 on it.

Why $5? Five dollars is an amount of money that is small yet not insignificant, and can really add up fast (20 questions could cost you $100). Likewise, each answer choice on one question of the test will have a small impact on your overall score, but it can really add up to a lot of points in the end.

The process of elimination IS valuable. The following shows your chance of guessing it right:

If you eliminate wrong answer choices until only this many remain:	Chance of getting it correct:
1	100%
2	50%
3	33%

However, if you accidentally eliminate the right answer or go on a hunch for an incorrect answer, your chances drop

dramatically: to 0%. By guessing among all the answer choices, you are GUARANTEED to have a shot at the right answer.

That's why the $5 test is so valuable- if you give up the advantage and safety of a pure guess, it had better be worth the risk.

What we still haven't covered is how to be sure that whatever guess you make is truly random. Here's the easiest way:

Always pick the first answer choice among those remaining.

Such a technique means that you have decided, **before you see a single test question**, exactly how you are going to guess- and since the order of choices tells you nothing about which one is correct, this guessing technique is perfectly random.

This section is not meant to scare you away from making educated guesses or eliminating choices- you just need to define when a choice is worth eliminating. The $5 test, along with a pre-defined random guessing strategy, is the best way to make sure you reap all of the benefits of guessing.

Secret Key #3 - Practice Smarter, Not Harder

Many test takers delay the test preparation process because they dread the awful amounts of practice time they think necessary to succeed on the test. We have refined an effective method that will take you only a fraction of the time.

There are a number of "obstacles" in your way to succeed. Among these are answering questions, finishing in time, and mastering test-taking strategies. All must be executed on the day of the test at peak performance, or your score will suffer. The test is a mental marathon that has a large impact on your future.

Just like a marathon runner, it is important to work your way up to the full challenge. So first you just worry about questions, and then time, and finally strategy:

Success Strategy

1. Find a good source for practice tests.
2. If you are willing to make a larger time investment, consider using more than one study guide- often the different approaches of multiple authors will help you "get" difficult concepts.
3. Take a practice test with no time constraints, with all study helps "open book." Take your time with questions and focus on applying strategies.
4. Take a practice test with time constraints, with all guides "open book."
5. Take a final practice test with no open material and time limits

If you have time to take more practice tests, just repeat step 5. By gradually exposing yourself to the full rigors of the test environment, you will condition your mind to the stress of test day and maximize your success.

Secret Key #4 - Prepare, Don't Procrastinate

Let me state an obvious fact: if you take the test three times, you will get three different scores. This is due to the way you feel on test day, the level of preparedness you have, and, despite the test writers' claims to the contrary, some tests WILL be easier for you than others.

Since your future depends so much on your score, you should maximize your chances of success. In order to maximize the likelihood of success, you've got to prepare in advance. This means taking practice tests and spending time learning the information and test taking strategies you will need to succeed.

Never take the test as a "practice" test, expecting that you can just take it again if you need to. Feel free to take sample tests on your own, but when you go to take the official test, be prepared, be focused, and do your best the first time!

Secret Key #5 - Test Yourself

Everyone knows that time is money. There is no need to spend too much of your time or too little of your time preparing for the test. You should only spend as much of your precious time preparing as is necessary for you to get the score you need.

Once you have taken a practice test under real conditions of time constraints, then you will know if you are ready for the test or not.

If you have scored extremely high the first time that you take the practice test, then there is not much point in spending countless hours studying. You are already there.

Benchmark your abilities by retaking

practice tests and seeing how much you have improved. Once you score high enough to guarantee success, then you are ready.

If you have scored well below where you need, then knuckle down and begin studying in earnest. Check your improvement regularly through the use of practice tests under real conditions. Above all, don't worry, panic, or give up. The key is perseverance!

Then, when you go to take the test, remain confident and remember how well you did on the practice tests. If you can score high enough on a practice test, then you can do the same on the real thing.

General Strategies

The most important thing you can do is to ignore your fears and jump into the test immediately- do not be overwhelmed by any strange-sounding terms. You have to jump into the test like jumping into a pool- all at once is the easiest way.

Make Predictions
As you read and understand the question, try to guess what the answer will be. Remember that several of the answer choices are wrong, and once you begin reading them, your mind will immediately become cluttered with answer choices designed to throw you off. Your mind is typically the most focused immediately after you have read the question and digested its contents. If you can, try to predict what the correct answer will be. You may be surprised at what you can predict.

Quickly scan the choices and see if your prediction is in the listed answer choices. If it is, then you can be quite confident that you have the right answer. It still won't hurt to check the other answer choices, but most of the time, you've got it!

Answer the Question
It may seem obvious to only pick answer choices that answer the question, but the test writers can create some excellent answer choices that are wrong. Don't pick an answer just because it sounds right, or you believe it to be true. It MUST answer the question. Once you've made your selection, always go back and check it against the question and make sure that you didn't misread the question, and the answer choice does answer the question posed.

Benchmark
After you read the first answer choice, decide if you think it sounds correct or not. If it doesn't, move on to the next answer choice. If it does, mentally mark that answer choice. This doesn't mean that you've definitely selected it as your answer choice, it just means that it's the best you've seen thus far. Go ahead and read the next choice. If the next choice is worse than the one you've already selected, keep going to the next answer choice. If the next choice is better than the choice you've already selected, mentally mark the new answer choice as your best guess.

The first answer choice that you select becomes your standard. Every other answer choice must be benchmarked against that standard. That choice is correct until proven otherwise by another answer choice beating it out. Once you've decided that no other answer choice seems as good, do one final check to ensure that your answer choice answers the question posed.

Valid Information
Don't discount any of the information provided in the question. Every piece of information may be necessary to determine the correct answer. None of

the information in the question is there to throw you off (while the answer choices will certainly have information to throw you off). If two seemingly unrelated topics are discussed, don't ignore either. You can be confident there is a relationship, or it wouldn't be included in the question, and you are probably going to have to determine what is that relationship to find the answer.

Avoid "Fact Traps"

Don't get distracted by a choice that is factually true. Your search is for the answer that answers the question. Stay focused and don't fall for an answer that is true but incorrect. Always go back to the question and make sure you're choosing an answer that actually answers the question and is not just a true statement. An answer can be factually correct, but it MUST answer the question asked. Additionally, two answers can both be seemingly correct, so be sure to read all of the answer choices, and make sure that you get the one that BEST answers the question.

Milk the Question

Some of the questions may throw you completely off. They might deal with a subject you have not been exposed to, or one that you haven't reviewed in years. While your lack of knowledge about the subject will be a hindrance, the question itself can give you many clues that will help you find the correct answer. Read the question carefully and look for clues. Watch particularly for adjectives and nouns describing difficult terms or words that you don't recognize. Regardless of if you completely understand a word or not, replacing it with a synonym either provided or one you more familiar with may help you to understand what the questions are asking. Rather than wracking your mind about specific detailed information concerning a difficult term or word, try to use mental substitutes that are easier to understand.

The Trap of Familiarity

Don't just choose a word because you recognize it. On difficult questions, you may not recognize a number of words in the answer choices. The test writers don't put "make-believe" words on the test; so don't think that just because you only recognize all the words in one answer choice means that answer choice must be correct. If you only recognize words in one answer choice, then focus on that one. Is it correct? Try your best to determine if it is correct. If it is, that is great, but if it doesn't, eliminate it. Each word and answer choice you eliminate increases your chances of getting the question correct, even if you then have to guess among the unfamiliar choices.

Eliminate Answers

Eliminate choices as soon as you realize they are wrong. But be careful! Make sure you consider all of the possible answer choices. Just because one appears right, doesn't mean that the next one won't be even better! The test writers will usually put more than one good answer choice for every question, so read all of them. Don't worry if you are stuck between two that seem right. By getting down to just two remaining possible choices, your odds are now 50/50. Rather than wasting too much time, play the odds. You are guessing, but guessing wisely, because you've been able to knock out some of the answer choices that you know are wrong. If you are eliminating choices and realize that the last answer choice you are left with is also obviously wrong, don't panic. Start over and consider each choice again. There may easily be something that you missed the first time and will realize on the second pass.

Tough Questions

If you are stumped on a problem or it appears too hard or too difficult, don't waste time. Move on! Remember though, if you can quickly check for obviously

- 125 -

incorrect answer choices, your chances of guessing correctly are greatly improved. Before you completely give up, at least try to knock out a couple of possible answers. Eliminate what you can and then guess at the remaining answer choices before moving on.

Brainstorm

If you get stuck on a difficult question, spend a few seconds quickly brainstorming. Run through the complete list of possible answer choices. Look at each choice and ask yourself, "Could this answer the question satisfactorily?" Go through each answer choice and consider it independently of the other. By systematically going through all possibilities, you may find something that you would otherwise overlook. Remember that when you get stuck, it's important to try to keep moving.

Read Carefully

Understand the problem. Read the question and answer choices carefully. Don't miss the question because you misread the terms. You have plenty of time to read each question thoroughly and make sure you understand what is being asked. Yet a happy medium must be attained, so don't waste too much time. You must read carefully, but efficiently.

Face Value

When in doubt, use common sense. Always accept the situation in the problem at face value. Don't read too much into it. These problems will not require you to make huge leaps of logic. The test writers aren't trying to throw you off with a cheap trick. If you have to go beyond creativity and make a leap of logic in order to have an answer choice answer the question, then you should look at the other answer choices. Don't overcomplicate the problem by creating theoretical relationships or explanations that will warp time or space. These are normal problems rooted in reality. It's

just that the applicable relationship or explanation may not be readily apparent and you have to figure things out. Use your common sense to interpret anything that isn't clear.

Prefixes

If you're having trouble with a word in the question or answer choices, try dissecting it. Take advantage of every clue that the word might include. Prefixes and suffixes can be a huge help. Usually they allow you to determine a basic meaning. Pre- means before, post- means after, pro - is positive, de- is negative. From these prefixes and suffixes, you can get an idea of the general meaning of the word and try to put it into context. Beware though of any traps. Just because con is the opposite of pro, doesn't necessarily mean congress is the opposite of progress!

Hedge Phrases

Watch out for critical "hedge" phrases, such as likely, may, can, will often, sometimes, often, almost, mostly, usually, generally, rarely, sometimes. Question writers insert these hedge phrases to cover every possibility. Often an answer choice will be wrong simply because it leaves no room for exception. Avoid answer choices that have definitive words like "exactly," and "always".

Switchback Words

Stay alert for "switchbacks". These are the words and phrases frequently used to alert you to shifts in thought. The most common switchback word is "but". Others include although, however, nevertheless, on the other hand, even though, while, in spite of, despite, regardless of.

New Information

Correct answer choices will rarely have completely new information included. Answer choices typically are straightforward reflections of the material asked about and will directly relate to the question. If a new piece of information is included in an answer choice that doesn't even seem to relate to the topic being asked about, then that answer choice is likely incorrect. All of the information needed to answer the question is usually provided for you, and so you should not have to make guesses that are unsupported or choose answer choices that require unknown information that cannot be reasoned on its own.

Time Management

On technical questions, don't get lost on the technical terms. Don't spend too much time on any one question. If you don't know what a term means, then since you don't have a dictionary, odds are you aren't going to get much further. You should immediately recognize terms as whether or not you know them. If you don't, work with the other clues that you have, the other answer choices and terms provided, but don't waste too much time trying to figure out a difficult term.

Contextual Clues

Look for contextual clues. An answer can be right but not correct. The contextual clues will help you find the answer that is most right and is correct. Understand the context in which a phrase or statement is made. This will help you make important distinctions.

Don't Panic

Panicking will not answer any questions for you. Therefore, it isn't helpful. When you first see the question, if your mind goes blank, take a deep breath. Force yourself to mechanically go through the steps of solving the problem and using the strategies you've learned.

Pace Yourself

Don't get clock fever. It's easy to be overwhelmed when you're looking at a page full of questions, your mind is full of random thoughts and feeling confused, and the clock is ticking down faster than you would like. Calm down and maintain the pace that you have set for yourself. As long as you are on track by monitoring your pace, you are guaranteed to have enough time for yourself. When you get to the last few minutes of the test, it may seem like you won't have enough time left, but if you only have as many questions as you should have left at that point, then you're right on track!

Answer Selection

The best way to pick an answer choice is to eliminate all of those that are wrong, until only one is left and confirm that is the correct answer. Sometimes though, an answer choice may immediately look right. Be careful! Take a second to make sure that the other choices are not equally obvious. Don't make a hasty mistake. There are only two times that you should stop before checking other answers. First is when you are positive that the answer choice you have selected is correct. Second is when time is almost out and you have to make a quick guess!

Check Your Work

Since you will probably not know every term listed and the answer to every question, it is important that you get credit for the ones that you do know. Don't miss any questions through careless mistakes. If at all possible, try to take a second to look back over your answer selection and make sure you've selected the correct answer choice and haven't made a costly careless mistake (such as marking an answer choice that you didn't mean to mark). This quick double check should more than pay for itself in caught mistakes for the time it costs.

Beware of Directly Quoted Answers

Sometimes an answer choice will repeat word for word a portion of the question or reference section. However, beware of such exact duplication – it may be a trap!

More than likely, the correct choice will paraphrase or summarize a point, rather than being exactly the same wording.

Slang
Scientific sounding answers are better than slang ones. An answer choice that begins "To compare the outcomes..." is much more likely to be correct than one that begins "Because some people insisted..."

Extreme Statements
Avoid wild answers that throw out highly controversial ideas that are proclaimed as established fact. An answer choice that states the "process should be used in certain situations, if..." is much more likely to be correct than one that states the "process should be discontinued completely." The first is a calm rational statement and doesn't even make a definitive, uncompromising stance, using a hedge word "if" to provide wiggle room, whereas the second choice is a radical idea and far more extreme.

Answer Choice Families
When you have two or more answer choices that are direct opposites or parallels, one of them is usually the correct answer. For instance, if one answer choice states "x increases" and another answer choice states "x decreases" or "y increases," then those two or three answer choices are very similar in construction and fall into the same family of answer choices. A family of answer choices is when two or three answer choices are very similar in construction, and yet often have a directly opposite meaning. Usually the correct answer choice will be in that family of answer choices. The "odd man out" or answer choice that doesn't seem to fit the parallel construction of the other answer choices is more likely to be incorrect.

Special Report: What Your Test Score Will Tell You About Your IQ

Did you know that most standardized tests correlate very strongly with IQ? In fact, your general intelligence is a better predictor of your success than any other factor, and most tests intentionally measure this trait to some degree to ensure that those selected by the test are truly qualified for the test's purposes.

Before we can delve into the relation between your test score and IQ, I will first have to explain what exactly is IQ. Here's the formula:

Your IQ = 100 + (Number of standard deviations below or above the average)*15

Now, let's define standard deviations by using an example. If we have 5 people with 5 different heights, then first we calculate the average. Let's say the average was 65 inches. The standard deviation is the "average distance" away from the average of each of the members. It is a direct measure of variability - if the 5 people included Jackie Chan and Shaquille O'Neal, obviously there's a lot more variability in that group than a group of 5 sisters who are all within 6 inches in height of each other. The standard deviation uses a number to characterize the average range of difference within a group.

A convenient feature of most groups is that they have a "normal" distribution- makes sense that most things would be normal, right? Without getting into a bunch of statistical mumbo-jumbo, you just need to know that if you know the average of the group and the standard deviation, you can successfully predict someone's percentile rank in the group.

Confused? Let me give you an example. If instead of 5 people's heights, we had 100 people, we could figure out their rank in height JUST by knowing the average, standard deviation, and their height. We wouldn't need to know each person's height and manually rank them, we could just predict their rank based on three numbers.

What this means is that you can take your PERCENTILE rank that is often given with your test and relate this to your RELATIVE IQ of people taking the test - that is, your IQ relative to the people taking the test. Obviously, there's no way to know your actual IQ because the people taking a standardized test are usually not very good samples of the general population- many of those with extremely low IQ's never achieve a level of success or competency necessary to complete a typical standardized test. In fact, professional psychologists who measure IQ actually have to use non-written tests that can fairly measure the IQ of those not able to complete a traditional test.

The bottom line is to not take your test score too seriously, but it is fun to compute your "relative IQ" among the people who took the test with you. I've done the calculations below. Just look up your percentile rank in the left and then you'll see your "relative IQ" for your test in the right hand column-

Percentile Rank	Your Relative IQ		Percentile Rank	Your Relative IQ
99	135		59	103
98	131		58	103
97	128		57	103
96	126		56	102
95	125		55	102
94	123		54	102
93	122		53	101
92	121		52	101
91	120		51	100
90	119		50	100
89	118		49	100
88	118		48	99
87	117		47	99
86	116		46	98
85	116		45	98
84	115		44	98
83	114		43	97
82	114		42	97
81	113		41	97
80	113		40	96
79	112		39	96
78	112		38	95
77	111		37	95
76	111		36	95
75	110		35	94
74	110		34	94
73	109		33	93
72	109		32	93
71	108		31	93
70	108		30	92
69	107		29	92
68	107		28	91
67	107		27	91
66	106		26	90
65	106		25	90
64	105		24	89
63	105		23	89
62	105		22	88
61	104		21	88
60	104		20	87

Special Report: What is Test Anxiety and How to Overcome It?

The very nature of tests caters to some level of anxiety, nervousness or tension, just as we feel for any important event that occurs in our lives. A little bit of anxiety or nervousness can be a good thing. It helps us with motivation, and makes achievement just that much sweeter. However, too much anxiety can be a problem; especially if it hinders our ability to function and perform.

"Test anxiety," is the term that refers to the emotional reactions that some test-takers experience when faced with a test or exam. Having a fear of testing and exams is based upon a rational fear, since the test-taker's performance can shape the course of an academic career. Nevertheless, experiencing excessive fear of examinations will only interfere with the test-takers ability to perform, and his/her chances to be successful.

There are a large variety of causes that can contribute to the development and sensation of test anxiety. These include, but are not limited to lack of performance and worrying about issues surrounding the test.

Lack of Preparation

Lack of preparation can be identified by the following behaviors or situations:

Not scheduling enough time to study, and therefore cramming the night before the test or exam
Managing time poorly, to create the sensation that there is not enough time to do everything
Failing to organize the text information in advance, so that the study material consists of the entire text and not simply the pertinent information
Poor overall studying habits

Worrying, on the other hand, can be related to both the test taker, or many other factors around him/her that will be affected by the results of the test. These include worrying about:

Previous performances on similar exams, or exams in general
How friends and other students are achieving
The negative consequences that will result from a poor grade or failure

There are three primary elements to test anxiety. Physical components, which involve the same typical bodily reactions as those to acute anxiety (to be discussed below). Emotional factors have to do with fear or panic. Mental or cognitive issues concerning attention spans and memory abilities.

Physical Signals

There are many different symptoms of test anxiety, and these are not limited to mental and emotional strain. Frequently there are a range of physical signals that will let a test taker know that he/she is suffering from test anxiety. These bodily changes can include the following:

Perspiring
Sweaty palms
Wet, trembling hands
Nausea
Dry mouth
A knot in the stomach
Headache
Faintness
Muscle tension
Aching shoulders, back and neck
Rapid heart beat
Feeling too hot/cold

To recognize the sensation of test anxiety, a test-taker should monitor him/herself for the following sensations:

The physical distress symptoms as listed above
Emotional sensitivity, expressing emotional feelings such as the need to cry or laugh too much, or a sensation of anger or helplessness
A decreased ability to think, causing the test-taker to blank out or have racing thoughts that are hard to organize or control.

Though most students will feel some level of anxiety when faced with a test or exam, the majority can cope with that anxiety and maintain it at a manageable level. However, those who cannot are faced with a very real and very serious condition, which can and should be controlled for the immeasurable benefit of this sufferer.

Naturally, these sensations lead to negative results for the testing experience. The most common effects of test anxiety have to do with nervousness and mental blocking.

Nervousness

Nervousness can appear in several different levels:

The test-taker's difficulty, or even inability to read and understand the questions on the test
The difficulty or inability to organize thoughts to a coherent form
The difficulty or inability to recall key words and concepts relating to the testing questions (especially essays)
The receipt of poor grades on a test, though the test material was well known by the test taker

Conversely, a person may also experience mental blocking, which involves:

Blanking out on test questions
Only remembering the correct answers to the questions when the test has already finished.

Fortunately for test anxiety sufferers, beating these feelings, to a large degree, has to do with proper preparation. When a test taker has a feeling of preparedness, then anxiety will be dramatically lessened.

The first step to resolving anxiety issues is to distinguish which of the two types of anxiety are being suffered. If the anxiety is a direct result of a lack of preparation, this should be considered a normal reaction, and the anxiety level (as opposed to the test results) shouldn't be anything to worry about. However, if, when adequately prepared, the test-taker still panics, blanks out, or seems to overreact, this is not a fully rational reaction. While this can be considered normal too, there are many ways to combat and overcome these effects.

Remember that anxiety cannot be entirely eliminated, however, there are ways to minimize it, to make the anxiety easier to manage. Preparation is one of the best ways to minimize test anxiety. Therefore the following techniques are wise in order to best fight off any anxiety that may want to build.

To begin with, try to avoid cramming before a test, whenever it is possible. By trying to memorize an entire term's worth of information in one day, you'll be shocking your system, and not giving yourself a very good chance to absorb the information. This is an easy path to anxiety, so for those who suffer from test anxiety, cramming should not even be considered an option.

Instead of cramming, work throughout the semester to combine all of the material which is presented throughout the semester, and work on it gradually as the course goes by, making sure to master the main concepts first, leaving minor details for a week or so before the test.

To study for the upcoming exam, be sure to pose questions that may be on the examination, to gauge the ability to answer them by integrating the ideas from your texts, notes and lectures, as well as any supplementary readings.

If it is truly impossible to cover all of the information that was covered in that particular term, concentrate on the most important portions, that can be covered very well. Learn these concepts as best as possible, so that when the test comes, a goal can be made to use these concepts as presentations of your knowledge.

In addition to study habits, changes in attitude are critical to beating a struggle with test anxiety. In fact, an improvement of the perspective over the entire test-taking experience can actually help a test taker to enjoy studying and therefore improve the overall experience. Be certain not to overemphasize the significance of the grade - know that the result of the test is neither a reflection of self worth, nor is it a measure of intelligence; one grade will not predict a person's future success.

To improve an overall testing outlook, the following steps should be tried:

Keeping in mind that the most reasonable expectation for taking a test is to expect to try to demonstrate as much of what you know as you possibly can.
Reminding ourselves that a test is only one test; this is not the only one, and there will be others.
The thought of thinking of oneself in an irrational, all-or-nothing term should be avoided at all costs.
A reward should be designated for after the test, so there's something to look forward to. Whether it be going to a movie, going out to eat, or simply visiting friends, schedule it in advance, and do it no matter what result is expected on the exam.

Test-takers should also keep in mind that the basics are some of the most important things, even beyond anti-anxiety techniques and studying. Never neglect the basic social, emotional and biological needs, in order to try to absorb information. In order to best achieve, these three factors must be held as just as important as the studying itself.

Study Steps

Remember the following important steps for studying:

Maintain healthy nutrition and exercise habits. Continue both your recreational activities and social pass times. These both contribute to your physical and emotional well being.
Be certain to get a good amount of sleep, especially the night before the test, because when you're overtired you are not able to perform to the best of your best ability.
Keep the studying pace to a moderate level by taking breaks when they are needed, and varying the work whenever possible, to keep the mind fresh instead of getting bored. When enough studying has been done that all the material that can be learned has been learned, and the test taker is prepared for the test, stop studying and do something relaxing such as listening to music, watching a movie, or taking a warm bubble bath.

There are also many other techniques to minimize the uneasiness or apprehension that is experienced along with test anxiety before, during, or even after the examination. In fact, there are a great deal of things that can be done to stop anxiety from interfering with lifestyle and performance. Again, remember that anxiety will not be eliminated entirely, and it shouldn't be. Otherwise that "up" feeling for exams would not exist, and most of us depend on that sensation to perform better than usual. However, this anxiety has to be at a level that is manageable.

Of course, as we have just discussed, being prepared for the exam is half the battle right away. Attending all classes, finding out what knowledge will be expected on the exam, and knowing the exam schedules are easy steps to lowering anxiety. Keeping up with work will remove the need to cram, and efficient study habits will eliminate wasted time. Studying should be done in an ideal location for concentration, so that it is simple to become interested in the material and give it complete attention. A method such as SQ3R (Survey, Question, Read, Recite, Review) is a wonderful key to follow to make sure that the study habits are as effective as possible, especially in the case of learning from a textbook. Flashcards are great techniques for memorization. Learning to take good notes will mean that notes will be full of useful information, so that less sifting will need to be done to seek out what is pertinent for studying. Reviewing notes after class and then again on occasion will keep the information fresh in the mind. From notes that have been taken summary sheets and outlines can be made for simpler reviewing.

A study group can also be a very motivational and helpful place to study, as there will be a sharing of ideas, all of the minds can work together, to make sure that everyone understands, and the studying will be made more interesting because it will be a social occasion.

Basically, though, as long as the test-taker remains organized and self confident, with efficient study habits, less time will need to be spent studying, and higher grades will be achieved.

To become self confident, there are many useful steps. The first of these is "self talk." It has been shown through extensive research, that self-talk for students who suffer from test anxiety, should be well monitored, in order to make sure that it contributes to self confidence as opposed to sinking the student. Frequently the self talk of test-anxious students is negative or self-defeating, thinking that everyone else is smarter and faster, that they always mess up, and that if they don't do well, they'll fail the entire course. It is important to decreasing anxiety that awareness is made of self talk. Try writing any negative self thoughts and then disputing them with a positive statement instead. Begin self-encouragement as though it was a friend speaking. Repeat positive statements to help reprogram the mind to believing in successes instead of failures.

Helpful Techniques

Other extremely helpful techniques include:

Self-visualization of doing well and reaching goals
While aiming for an "A" level of understanding, don't try to "overprotect" by setting your expectations lower. This will only convince the mind to stop studying in order to meet the lower expectations.
Don't make comparisons with the results or habits of other students. These are individual factors, and different things work for different people, causing different results.
Strive to become an expert in learning what works well, and what can be done in order to improve. Consider collecting this data in a journal.
Create rewards for after studying instead of doing things before studying that will only turn into avoidance behaviors.
Make a practice of relaxing - by using methods such as progressive relaxation, self-hypnosis, guided imagery, etc - in order to make relaxation an automatic sensation.
Work on creating a state of relaxed concentration so that concentrating will take on the focus of the mind, so that none will be wasted on worrying.
Take good care of the physical self by eating well and getting enough sleep.
Plan in time for exercise and stick to this plan.

Beyond these techniques, there are other methods to be used before, during and after the test that will help the test-taker perform well in addition to overcoming anxiety.

Before the exam comes the academic preparation. This involves establishing a study schedule and beginning at least one week before the actual date of the test. By doing this, the anxiety of not having enough time to study for the test will be automatically eliminated. Moreover, this will make the studying a much more effective experience, ensuring that the learning will be an easier process. This relieves much undue pressure on the test-taker.

Summary sheets, note cards, and flash cards with the main concepts and examples of these main concepts should be prepared in advance of the actual studying time. A topic should never be eliminated from this process. By omitting a topic because it isn't expected to be on the test is only setting up the test-taker for anxiety should it actually appear on the exam. Utilize the course syllabus for laying out the topics that should be studied. Carefully go over the notes that were made in class, paying special attention to any of the issues that the professor took special care to emphasize while lecturing in class. In the textbooks, use the chapter review, or if possible, the chapter tests, to begin your review.

It may even be possible to ask the instructor what information will be covered on the exam, or what the format of the exam will be (for example, multiple choice, essay, free form, true-false). Additionally, see if it is possible to find out how many questions will be on the test. If a review sheet or sample test has been offered by the professor, make good use of it, above anything else, for the preparation for the test. Another great resource for getting to know the examination is reviewing tests from previous semesters. Use these tests to review, and aim to achieve a 100% score on each of the possible topics. With a few exceptions, the goal that you set for yourself is the highest one that you will reach.

Take all of the questions that were assigned as homework, and rework them to any other possible course material. The more problems reworked, the more skill and confidence will form as a result. When forming the solution to a problem, write out each of the steps. Don't simply do head work. By doing as many steps on paper as possible, much clarification and therefore confidence will be formed. Do this with as many homework problems as possible, before checking the answers. By checking the answer after each problem, a reinforcement will exist, that will not be on the exam. Study situations should be as exam-like as possible, to prime the test-taker's system for the experience. By waiting to check the answers at the end, a psychological advantage will be formed, to decrease the stress factor.

Another fantastic reason for not cramming is the avoidance of confusion in concepts, especially when it comes to mathematics. 8-10 hours of study will become one hundred percent more effective if it is spread out over a week or at least several days, instead of doing it all in one sitting. Recognize that the human brain requires time in order to assimilate new material, so frequent breaks and a span of study time over several days will be much more beneficial.

Additionally, don't study right up until the point of the exam. Studying should stop a minimum of one hour before the exam begins. This allows the brain to rest and put things in their proper order. This will also provide the time to become as relaxed as possible when going into the examination room. The test-taker will also have time to eat well and eat sensibly. Know that the brain needs food as much as the rest of the body. With enough food and enough sleep, as well as a relaxed attitude, the body and the mind are primed for success.

Avoid any anxious classmates who are talking about the exam. These students only spread anxiety, and are not worth sharing the anxious sentimentalities.

Before the test also involves creating a positive attitude, so mental preparation should also be a point of concentration. There are many keys to creating a positive attitude. Should fears become rushing in, make a visualization of taking the exam, doing well, and seeing an A written on the paper. Write out a list of affirmations that will bring a feeling of confidence, such as "I am doing well in my English class," "I studied well and know my material," "I enjoy this class." Even if the affirmations aren't believed at first, it sends a positive message to the subconscious which will result in an alteration of the overall belief system, which is the system that creates reality.

If a sensation of panic begins, work with the fear and imagine the very worst! Work through the entire scenario of not passing the test, failing the entire course, and dropping out of school, followed by not getting a job, and pushing a shopping cart through the dark alley where you'll live. This will place things into perspective! Then, practice deep breathing and create a visualization of the opposite situation - achieving an "A" on the exam, passing the entire course, receiving the degree at a graduation ceremony.

On the day of the test, there are many things to be done to ensure the best results, as well as the most calm outlook. The following stages are suggested in order to maximize test-taking potential:

Begin the examination day with a moderate breakfast, and avoid any coffee or beverages with caffeine if the test taker is prone to jitters. Even people who are used to managing caffeine can feel jittery or light-headed when it is taken on a test day.
Attempt to do something that is relaxing before the examination begins. As last minute cramming clouds the mastering of overall concepts, it is better to use this time to create a calming outlook.
Be certain to arrive at the test location well in advance, in order to provide time to select a location that is away from doors, windows and other distractions, as well as giving enough time to relax before the test begins.
Keep away from anxiety generating classmates who will upset the sensation of stability and relaxation that is being attempted before the exam.
Should the waiting period before the exam begins cause anxiety, create a self-distraction by reading a light magazine or something else that is relaxing and simple.

During the exam itself, read the entire exam from beginning to end, and find out how much time should be allotted to each individual problem. Once writing the exam, should more time be taken for a problem, it should be abandoned, in order to begin another problem. If there is time at the end, the unfinished problem can always be returned to and completed.

Read the instructions very carefully - twice - so that unpleasant surprises won't follow during or after the exam has ended.

When writing the exam, pretend that the situation is actually simply the completion of homework within a library, or at home. This will assist in forming a relaxed atmosphere, and will allow the brain extra focus for the complex thinking function.

Begin the exam with all of the questions with which the most confidence is felt. This will build the confidence level regarding the entire exam and will begin a quality momentum. This will also create encouragement for trying the problems where uncertainty resides.

Going with the "gut instinct" is always the way to go when solving a problem. Second guessing should be avoided at all costs. Have confidence in the ability to do well.

For essay questions, create an outline in advance that will keep the mind organized and make certain that all of the points are remembered. For multiple choice, read every answer, even if the correct one has been spotted - a better one may exist.

Continue at a pace that is reasonable and not rushed, in order to be able to work carefully. Provide enough time to go over the answers at the end, to check for small errors that can be corrected.

Should a feeling of panic begin, breathe deeply, and think of the feeling of the body releasing sand through its pores. Visualize a calm, peaceful place, and include all of the sights, sounds and sensations of this image. Continue the deep breathing, and take a few minutes to continue this with closed eyes. When all is well again, return to the test.

If a "blanking" occurs for a certain question, skip it and move on to the next question. There will be time to return to the other question later. Get everything done that can be done, first, to guarantee all the grades that can be compiled, and to build all of the confidence possible. Then return to the weaker questions to build the marks from there.

Remember, one's own reality can be created, so as long as the belief is there, success will follow. And remember: anxiety can happen later, right now, there's an exam to be written!

After the examination is complete, whether there is a feeling for a good grade or a bad grade, don't dwell on the exam, and be certain to follow through on the reward that was promised...and enjoy it! Don't dwell on any mistakes that have been made, as there is nothing that can be done at this point anyway.

Additionally, don't begin to study for the next test right away. Do something relaxing for a while, and let the mind relax and prepare itself to begin absorbing information again.

From the results of the exam - both the grade and the entire experience, be certain to learn from what has gone on. Perfect studying habits and work some more on confidence in order to make the next examination experience even better than the last one.

Learn to avoid places where openings occurred for laziness, procrastination and day dreaming.

Use the time between this exam and the next one to better learn to relax, even learning to relax on cue, so that any anxiety can be controlled during the next exam. Learn how to relax the body. Slouch in your chair if that helps. Tighten and then relax all of the different muscle groups, one group at a time, beginning with the feet and then working all the way up to the neck and face. This will ultimately relax the muscles more than they were to begin with. Learn how to breathe deeply and comfortably, and focus on this breathing going in and out as a relaxing thought. With every exhale, repeat the word "relax."

As common as test anxiety is, it is very possible to overcome it. Make yourself one of the test-takers who overcome this frustrating hindrance.

Special Report: Retaking the Test: What Are Your Chances at Improving Your Score?

After going through the experience of taking a major test, many test takers feel that once is enough. The test usually comes during a period of transition in the test taker's life, and taking the test is only one of a series of important events. With so many distractions and conflicting recommendations, it may be difficult for a test taker to rationally determine whether or not he should retake the test after viewing his scores.

The importance of the test usually only adds to the burden of the retake decision. However, don't be swayed by emotion. There a few simple questions that you can ask yourself to guide you as you try to determine whether a retake would improve your score:

1. What went wrong? Why wasn't your score what you expected?

Can you point to a single factor or problem that you feel caused the low score? Were you sick on test day? Was there an emotional upheaval in your life that caused a distraction? Were you late for the test or not able to use the full time allotment? If you can point to any of these specific, individual problems, then a retake should definitely be considered.

2. Is there enough time to improve?

Many problems that may show up in your score report may take a lot of time for improvement. A deficiency in a particular math skill may require weeks or months of tutoring and studying to improve. If you have enough time to improve an identified weakness, then a retake should definitely be considered.

3. How will additional scores be used? Will a score average, highest score, or most recent score be used?

Different test scores may be handled completely differently. If you've taken the test multiple times, sometimes your highest score is used, sometimes your average score is computed and used, and sometimes your most recent score is used. Make sure you understand what method will be used to evaluate your scores, and use that to help you determine whether a retake should be considered.

4. Are my practice test scores significantly higher than my actual test score?

If you have taken a lot of practice tests and are consistently scoring at a much higher level than your actual test score, then you should consider a retake. However, if you've taken five practice tests and only one of your scores was higher than your actual test score, or if your practice test scores were only slightly higher than your actual test score, then it is unlikely that you will significantly increase your score.

5. Do I need perfect scores or will I be able to live with this score? Will this score still allow me to follow my dreams?

What kind of score is acceptable to you? Is your current score "good enough?" Do you have to have a certain score in order to pursue the future of your dreams? If you won't be happy with your current score, and there's no way that you could live with it, then you should consider a retake. However, don't get your hopes up. If you are looking for significant improvement, that may or may not be possible. But if you won't be happy otherwise, it is at least worth the effort.
Remember that there are other considerations. To achieve your dream, it is likely that your grades may also be taken into account. A great test score is usually not the only thing necessary to succeed. Make sure that you aren't overemphasizing the importance of a high test score.

Furthermore, a retake does not always result in a higher score. Some test takers will score lower on a retake, rather than higher. One study shows that one-fourth of test takers will achieve a significant improvement in test score, while one-sixth of test takers will actually show a decrease. While this shows that most test takers will improve, the majority will only improve their scores a little and a retake may not be worth the test taker's effort.

Finally, if a test is taken only once and is considered in the added context of good grades on the part of a test taker, the person reviewing the grades and scores may be tempted to assume that the test taker just had a bad day while taking the test, and may discount the low test score in favor of the high grades. But if the test is retaken and the scores are approximately the same, then the validity of the low scores are only confirmed. Therefore, a retake could actually hurt a test taker by definitely bracketing a test taker's score ability to a limited range.

Special Report: Additional Bonus Material

Due to our efforts to try to keep this book to a manageable length, we've created a link that will give you access to all of your additional bonus material.

Please visit http://www.mometrix.com/bonus948/nesincapkelem to access the information.